ADVANCED PRAISE FOR *ZUGUNRUHE*
THE INNER MIGRATION TO PROFOUND ENVIRONMENTAL CHANGE

"What Jason McLennan does in his powerful new book is to shift our focus on sustainability from technology to the heart of what it's all about: our personal and collective journey that will change our design practices, our culture and our way of life. His presentation is practical, passionate, and positive. Funny, and filled with useful stories and gems of advice. The best road map I've seen to join on our journey together."

—SIM VAN DER RYN, architect, visionary and author, *Design For Life, Ecological Design, Ecological Design* and *Sustainable Communities.*

"A true warrior cuts through his story and steps forth from his vision. Jason F. McLennan exposes the misperceptions, bad habits, and justifications that keep us at war with our earth. He presents a blueprint for a courageous, peaceful, and nurturing relationship with our planet. Heed this green warrior's words, and act – the world needs you."

—THOMAS CRUM, author, *The Magic of Conflict, Journey to Center* and *Three Deep Breaths*

"*Zugunruhe* is a work of creative genius that draws us into an engaging journey of self-discovery, brings the biggest and most frightening issues of our time up close and personal, evokes our inner courage, and invites our engagement in an epic creative challenge. It will leave you envisioning human possibilities you never previously imagined."

—DAVID KORTEN, co-founder and board chair of YES! Magazine and author, *Agenda for a New Economy: From Phantom Wealth to Real Wealth, The Great Turning: From Empire to Earth Community,* and *When Corporations Rule the World.*

"Whether you are just awakening to an inner calling to be the change you want to see in the world or have been at it for as long as you can remember, you will find valuable insights and pearls of wisdom from a visionary focused on the relationships between human beings, human doings and the built and natural worlds."

—DAVID EISENBERG, Director of the Development Center for Appropriate Technology (DCAT)

"A delicious meal of truths and insights about the world we have and the world we want seasoned with lessons from the life of a true green warrior— *Zugunruhe* shines a light on a hidden axiom of sustainability. Our hope lies in our connection to our innermost selves and to each other"

—SANDY WIGGINS, Principal, Consilience LLC.

"Even if you don't totally agree with Jason's opinions—and *especially* if you don't—you won't be able to deny the fact that Jason's words ring absolutely true. His opinions will provoke you, his personal stories will inspire you, and hopefully his book will prompt you to act with all the urgency you can muster. Required reading for anyone who desires a future that our children and grandchildren can thrive in."

—KATHLEEN O'BRIEN, CEO, O'Brien and Associates

"Jason is a brilliant synthesizer of ideas, creating frameworks that shift the conversation. Now he offers an inside look at the stories and experiences behind those big ideas, enriching the conversation even further."

—NADAV MALIN, President, Building Green, LLC

"*Zugunruhe* is a great read for anyone experiencing a lack of success in redefining design and community, or seeking better strategies for the 21st Century. This is Jason F. McLennan's personal story as an architect and green warrior—a roadmap for transformation, adaptation, inspiration and change—a guide for expressing love at the community scale."

—BOB BERKEBILE, FAIA – BNIM Architects

"This is an absolutely fabulous book! *Zugunruhe* is a very personal journey of discovery and a powerful invitation to begin our own journeys to make a real difference in the world."

—DR. JOHN FRANCIS, author, *Planetwalker: How to Change Your World One Step at a Time*

"The coming global transformation begins as we transform ourselves. As Jason McLennan explains, transformation works inside out. The century ahead will require stamina, wisdom, and courage, the prerequisites for which are inner clarity, depth, and compassion. Tall order. But the necessary instructions, mentors, and exemplars are all around us from the hummingbird to the heroes and heroines living down the street. *Zugunruhe*—migratory restlessness—is in the air. Jason McLennan beckons us to the journey ahead with a combination of wisdom, humor, practical good sense, and inspiration."

—DAVID W. ORR, Distinguished Professor of Environmental Studies and Politics at Oberlin College, author of *Down to the Wire - Confronting Climate Collapse, Design on the Edge* and *The Last Refuge*

"Jason McLennan, a brilliant, influential pioneer who works and lives on the sharpest edge of green design, turns deeply personal and reflective in "Zugunruhe." I view this book as the very antithesis of the memoirs of another influential architect whose reach extended far beyond buildings: Albert Speer. Unlike Speer, Jason reflects on why and how he does good – not evil."

DENIS HAYES, *Founder of Earth Day*

Also by Jason F. McLennan:

The Dumb Architect's Guide to Glazing
The Philosophy of Sustainable Design
The Ecological Engineer

tsʊk'ʊn-rū'he

ZUGUNRUHE

The Inner Migration To Profound Environmental Change

JASON F. MCLENNAN

WITH MARY ADAM THOMAS

FOREWORD BY
JANINE BENYUS

ECOtone LLC
publishing company

Copyright © 2011 by Ecotone Publishing

For more information write:
Ecotone Publishing
3187 Point White Drive NE
Bainbridge Island, WA 98110

Author: Jason F. McLennan
Book Design: softfirm
Edited by: Fred McLennan

Library of Congress Control Number: 2010924419

Library of Congress Cataloging-in Publication Data

ISBN 978-0-9749033-2-3

1. Environment   2. Green Building   3. Self-help

First Edition

Printed in Canada on Reincarnation Matte paper – one hundred percent
recycled content, Processed Chlorine-Free, using vegetable-based ink.

ABOUT ECOTONE PUBLISHING
THE GREEN BUILDING PUBLISHER

Ecotone Publishing – exploring the relationship between the built and natural environments

Founded and operated by green building experts, Ecotone Publishing is the first book publisher to focus solely on green architecture and design. Headquartered on Bainbridge Is., WA, the company is dedicated to meeting the growing demand for authoritative and accessible books on sustainable design, materials selection and building techniques in North America and beyond. Ecotone institutes a variety of green strategies, including the printing of its books on recycled content paper with vegetable-based inks, the use of recyclable packaging and supporting employees telecommuting from home offices. Ecotone proudly supports environmental and social organizations through collaboration, partnership and membership. An industry leader, Ecotone is the first American publishing company to fully adopt carbon neutrality to its business practices, in order to offset its own contributions to climate change.

Our commitment to the environment and to a sustainable future is the driving force behind every action we undertake.

www.ecotonedesign.com

ENVIRONMENTAL BENEFITS STATEMENT

ECOtone Publishing LLC saved the following resources by printing the pages of this book on chlorine free paper made with 100% post-consumer waste.

TREES	WATER	SOLID WASTE	GREENHOUSE GASES
14	**6,303**	**383**	**1,309**
FULLY GROWN	GALLONS	POUNDS	POUNDS

Calculations based on research by Environmental Defense and the Paper Task Force. Manufactured at Friesens Corporation

DEDICATION

This book is dedicated to my Mother and Father – Sandra and Fred McLennan, who have done more than anyone to prepare me for my own inner migration. How can you ever properly thank two people who have given, loved and supported so much, for so long, unconditionally?

While it is wholly insufficient, this book is for them – with all the love I can muster.

—Jason F. McLennan, 2010

TABLE OF CONTENTS

ACKNOWLEDGMENTS

The creation of Zugunruhe was a long process that occurred over a four-year period. During that time I had help from many individuals too numerous to mention but whose thoughts and ideas I greatly appreciate. To start out I wish to thank the whole team at Cascadia – both staff and board for what they bring to the green building movement each day – thank you all!

A big thank you goes out to my manuscript reviewers, that included a powerful list of leaders (in no particular order) Sim Van Der Ryn, Dr. John Francis, Bob Berkebile, Kath Williams, David Eisenberg, Kathleen O'Brien, Sandy Wiggins, David Orr, Nadav Malin, Pliny Fisk III, Thomas Crum and David Korten. Their insights and willingness to offer words of wisdom and testimony was vital.

A special heartfelt thank you hug goes to Janine Benyus who was kind enough to write the Foreword to the book on her scant vacation time – you are wonderful Janine!

To the book production crew and team at Ecotone – what would I do without you? This includes Mike Berrisford for his words of encouragement and marketing savvy, Fred McLennan – the world's best editor, Erin Gehle, my amazing graphic designer and, of course, Mary Thomas who made this book possible despite my schedule – a big heartfelt thank you!

Always providing inspiration and support are my wonderful children – Julian, Declan, Aidan and Rowan. They are the reason

I do this stuff – and my wonderful wife Tracy who keeps it all together and teaches me to be a more patient person – you guys are the real inspiration in my life!

Finally, a quiet and anonymous thank you to two groups - all those who have trickled in looking for answers – yet content to leave without most of them! You are the reason I wrote this book and I hope it is useful in your personal Zugunruhe! And to the many greenwarriors who inspired so much of what is in these pages (look for their names inside and you will know they are the ones I am speaking of here) – without you I would have nothing worthwhile to print. Thank you for preparing me for my own journey.

Much Love,

Jason F. McLennan

TRIBUTE TO MARY ADAM THOMAS

As I began this book I had the good fortune to meet Mary Thomas while riding my bike with my kids the first summer after just having moved to Bainbridge Island. It was serendipity at its finest. For some reason in our very short conversation the topic of writing came up and I had a feeling we were going to collaborate on something.

A few months later we happened to speak again and I asked her to help me with this project. Mary is a gifted writer, editor and mind reader who helped me refine and focus many of my ideas – and perhaps most importantly, had the discipline to see this project through to completion in the midst of my travels, commitments and daily chaos. Without Mary this book would not be what it is.

Thank you Mary!

FOREWORD BY JANINE BENYUS

AUTHOR, BIOMIMICRY: INNOVATION INSPIRED BY NATURE

The Montana dusk is broken by a call, booming and sonorous, that my cats and I have nearly forgotten. We look up in unison, then pour from the house to scan the salmon and silver sunset. Our neighbors are out too, hushing their spooked horses. We wave urgently to one another and pantomime a ten-foot wingspan.

"Sandhills!"

You hear sandhill cranes long before you see them. Their rolling call, amplified by a french-horn-shaped windpipe, is one of the loudest and most complex in the avian clan. On lucky evenings like this, their communiqués roll like waves round the glacial bowl that holds our home.

The first calls, from cranes hidden in head-high grasses, mean: "Good feeding here! It's worth a stopover." Those aloft (also invisible to us) return the chorus, and within minutes, a phalanx of pterodactyls appears, gliding down the sky to our pastures and ponds. Just like that, our valley is alive with gossiping, feasting birds comparing notes on their southern migration.

Without their ability to communicate over long distances, the choreography of a sandhill migration would be broken, and the birds that need one another for safe and fatigue-free flight would literally be lost. But this flock is in perfect sync. After a few days of fattening, it's time to go again, and the urge becomes visible in their agitated rustling. With every move, they telegraph a desire for warmer climes and more dependable hunting grounds. Wanderlust spreads through the flock like a contagion you can see.

Biologists call this migratory restlessness "zugunruhe," and Jason F. McLennan sees this urge in his colleagues as well. "So many people come up to me and want to leave perfectly good jobs," he tells me, "They're dissatisfied with the pace of environmental progress, and feel they can no longer fiddle while Rome burns." I know what he means, because I see it in the folks who apply for jobs at the Biomimicry Guild. We call it 'leaving to join the circus,' masking with humor what we know to be a growing truth. People feel a phase change in the air, and they know that the most audacious challenges humans have ever faced can't be left to the next generation, or to some other culture or profession. Saving the planet is not something you can outsource, because the scope of the work is too enormous, and the consequences of failure too unthinkable. It takes all of us to save a planet, and it takes each of us aspiring to a heightened state of self- and other-awareness. It takes maturity to be a welcome species.

My life intersected with Jason's the moment I opened an article that he and Bob Berkebile had written shortly after my book on biomimicry came out. The 'Living Building' title rocked me because at that time, the notion of a building as anything other than a high-performance machine was not common parlance. When I read that their mentor was a flower (a flower!), I was cheering from my chair. They built their argument on an obvious but subtle truth—that a flower can't run away, which makes it a model for how to deal gracefully and ingeniously with the realities—the opportunities as well as the limits   of your habitat. I tipped my biologist hat. As I turned the page, I was truly humbled to find that these sages from Kansas City had included quotes from my book. Suddenly I realized, in a way I hadn't before, how closely interconnected we are in this new journey to a better world. We are each other's mentors. These authors, for whom I felt such respect, had actually woven some of my thinking into their thinking. We are all creating this path as we travel it, I thought out loud. Which makes what we say, write, and do doubly resonant. We're in a flock of journeyers, and we learn from each other how to find the way home.

Jason decided to serve our flock long ago, learning from a coworker who never complained about a broken system, but instead became whatever his community required. When the department needed to sharpen their computer skills, he learned the ropes himself and brought technology to the community. Jason's done the same for green building.

When he realized that the LEED building standard was becoming mainstream, he crafted the next stretch-goal for early adopters—the Living Building Challenge. When he realized that no "nutritional label" existed for building materials, he didn't curse its lack, but instead created Pharos, pulling it from the oven "¾ baked" so others could take it from there. And when he realized that we "green warriors" are scattered and in need of community, he created a vibrant web presence, and a truly heartful annual conference called Living Future.

And now, with this communiqué, Jason comes straight from his heart to ours. In a sea of books about lumens, negawatts, slow money, and fast companies, he writes instead about telling the truth, leading with love, banishing doubt, and mastering the art of letting go. It's a checklist for our maiden journey, a personal to-do list for our migration to a better world.

When I'm in the cacophony of conferences like Living Future, I'll sometimes freeze-frame the action, turn down the sound, and breathe it all in. Seeing arms draped around shoulders, hands clapped in laughter, minds melding in hallways, and tears falling in plenary talks, I realize that *this* is how it happens. It's not someone else who will be the change, or rewrite the human story for us. We're the ones who've decided to pull together as a species and start moving toward the common good.

The windpipes of sandhills are designed for collaboration, and even their physiology morphs in unison before a strenuous trip. Birds that spend all year in ones or twos become uncommonly social. They grow new flight feathers, search for bountiful pastures, and shift sleep patterns so they're ready to fly all night. Even cranes in captivity show solidarity, orienting flight paths to the movements of wild flocks.

Somehow they know, as we do, that it's time to spread their wings. The world that they, and we, have been dreaming about is waiting.

– Janine Benyus
   Stevensville, Montana

GWERSI

In the ancient Celtic Welsh language the word for a "lesson" is Gwers and for a series of "Lessons" – Gwersi.

I have adopted these names for the short poem-like "essence-lessons" that I draw throughout this book.

ZUGUNRUHE

FINDING YOUR PATH TO PROFOUND CHANGE IN THE SUSTAINABILITY MOVEMENT

Your reason and passion are the rudder and the sails of your seafaring soul. If either your sails or your rudder be broken, you can but toss and drift, or else be held at a standstill in mid-seas. For reason, ruling alone is a force confining: and passion, unattended, is a flame that burns to its own destruction.

—Kahlil Gibran

THE HUMMINGBIRD

When I was a little boy, I used to look in wonder at the tiny little hummingbirds that flocked to my mother's feeder outside our window. They were small and delicate and able to hover almost as if by magic, with wings beating so fast as to be nearly invisible.

How did they do that?

As I grew a little older in my northern Ontario home, the wonder only increased as I learned that this tiny creature weighing only as much as a penny would set out each fall on a dangerous journey of more than 1500 miles to its winter grounds in Mexico. Along the way, the hummingbird faces numerous perils including a herculean crossing of the Gulf of Mexico in a single non-stop burst of exertion that lasts up to twenty hours. These birds are so small and carry so few reserves that any extra delay proves fatal. Knowing the right time to migrate and the right time to cross is fundamental to its survival. Sensing changes in air pressure hundreds of miles away, hummingbirds routinely avoid the deadliest storms that could easily spell the end of their journey and their lives. Would that we could predict such storms at the outset of our journeys – our migrations.

No less impressive are the hundreds of other species of birds and mammals that brave hostile conditions to migrate and set out on voyages back and forth across countries and whole continents. Imagine the changes witnessed each year by Arctic Terns that travel 22,000 miles from North to South Pole and back each year, or the great wildebeests that travel en masse in a thunderous cacophony (and nearly two million strong) from one biome to another following the emergence of rains and grasses.

At the right time, taking cues from changes in their environments, including temperature, length of day and night, food and water availability and other factors that we do not yet understand, all of these animals begin a restless transformation as they prepare for their journey. Pending changes in their environment trigger noticeable changes in their behavior; they consume greater amounts of food and alter their sleeping and other patterns, all as part of a physiological response to what is happening around them. As the winds change and conditions non-conducive to life begin to emerge, these animals respond and prepare to stay one step ahead – they sense the urgency and, through instinct, they prepare to migrate.

If we once shared such prescience as a species it no longer shows. Great calamitous changes are afoot in the global environment and in every regional and local ecosystem on every continent and yet the majority of humanity goes on like it has for decades – not altering its behavior in response to these changes – nor preparing for the figurative migration that all of us will soon be forced to begin.

Or is this the complete truth?

Is it possible that many of us are unconsciously preparing and have been for some time? People who were previously unconnected with the environmental movement are slowly becoming aware of the change, restless and soon to join the growing mutual flock.

BEGINNINGS OF A JOURNEY

In early 2006, I did what some people might consider a crazy thing: I initiated my own seemingly bizarre migration. I quit my job in Kansas City, where I was the youngest partner (the next youngest was twelve years my senior) in a nationally prominent architectural firm (BNIM Architects[1]). I took a pay cut, moved to a significantly more expensive place (Seattle) and started work as the CEO of a non-profit (the

---

[1] Architects www.bnim.com.

Cascadia Region Green Building Council[2] focused on green building advocacy) in a professional environment that differed completely from the for-profit world with which I was familiar. I did it with a growing young family in tow; my wife and I drove cross-country by van with three young children, a Great Dane and all of our belongings, trading stability for something I believed I had to do.

For several years prior to the move, I had felt restless for reasons I could not quite define, even though my career in architecture was blossoming and I was fortunate enough to work on some of the most important "green" architectural commissions anywhere on the continent. I have always been involved in environmental issues since my childhood growing up in Sudbury – a community infamous in environmental circles due to the devastating impacts of the mining industry – and equally well-known for its United Nations recognized re-greening process in which I participated as a child. And from graduation through my time at BNIM, my work always focused on designing energy and resource efficient buildings.

In the mid-nineties I started out as Bob Berkebile's[3] right-hand man – and just a few short years later ended up as his partner in a dynamic firm of one hundred professionals working on projects ranging in size from a couple of thousand to several hundred thousand square feet. Bob was and is my mentor and friend, and one of the most important contributors to the growth of the green building movement in the United States. I had the great fortune of working with him on some of the greenest projects anywhere – from LEED Platinum and Gold buildings to net zero energy homes and community designs. And yet, as each building got built, regardless of how green it was, I could not shake the feeling that I was not doing enough to create the level of

---

[2] www.cascadiagbc.org

[3] Berkebile is the 'B' in BNIM – one of the founding partners of the firm.

change needed in the environment. That somehow for all the good we were doing, we were failing to be where we should be.

And so my restlessness grew, and despite having "made-it" according to the architectural world's traditional benchmarks, I gave it all up. I packed up my family and drove west from the Midwest to the Pacific Northwest, into the heart of the growing green building movement, and joined Cascadia as its new CEO.

My timing turned out to be auspicious, for great changes in the green building and environmental worlds were happening simultaneously.

After more than two decades of being a fringe subset of the building industry with slow growth, the green building movement began growing by leaps and bounds as the '90s transitioned into the year 2000, with each successive year seeing huge growth. But in 2006 the movement took a giant leap forward and suddenly "green" was everywhere.

THE SHIFT

In my opinion, 2006 was the year when the green building movement moved into the mainstream consciousness[4] and the level of awareness and interest took on a whole new dimension. There was an invisible tipping point; suddenly LEED buildings were everywhere and environmental awareness, strengthened by the shock of Katrina in 2005 and the popularity of Al Gore's Oscar-winning movie "An Inconvenient Truth," reached audiences in ways environmentalists had been hoping to do for years. The issue of climate change in particular finally began to get people's attention and the feeling of urgency began to creep into common discussion and in magazines as unrelated as *Sports Illustrated* and *Fortune*.

---

[4] Although it is fair to say that "green" is still not mainstream in actual practice.

As "the winds" began changing while I settled into my new job, I quickly learned that I was not alone in my personal migration. People from all walks of life were trying to figure out how they could make more of a difference; how they could contribute to helping solve the greatest crises imaginable – changes to climate that could undermine our very civilization. Out of the blue, many of these people began finding me. Within a couple of months after I came to Cascadia, I was surprised by people seeking me out to get career advice, who under normal circumstances, would never seek to – doctors, engineers, builders, marketing professionals, product manufacturers, teachers, nurses, bankers – people from a diverse and divergent background coming to me and asking for guidance about how to rededicate themselves to the green effort!

I found this perplexing at first – what did I have to share? I was no career counselor! What did I know about telling a doctor or a lawyer how to get into the world of sustainability?

I did not presume to know what people should do with their professional lives. After all, I was a designer... I could tell you how to save energy and water but these people all wanted to talk about their desire to change who they were and what they did with their time and life energy.

So I mostly listened.

I let them talk about what they wanted to talk about and I asked them questions about what they cared about and why they felt they needed to change professions or to change the way they already practiced in whatever industry they were from. The common currency was that each thought – no – felt something was profoundly wrong with the environment and they were compelled to try, even in small ways, to do something about it. These people, to a person, seemed "restless" and agitated – in my view it seemed that they were reacting to environmental signals happening all around them. Signals that told them that change was coming and that they needed to be prepared.

I recall a physician who told me that even though he worked on incredibly important cancer research, he believed it was the state of the environment that was the root cause – and that it was the environment that he should concentrate on.

I talked to a fashion photographer who wanted to help educate parents on how to opt out of the typical consumer trap that is part of raising so many kids; a public relations professional who wanted to do her part to fight greenwash so people could make better decisions; a manufactured building company owner who wanted to make everything he touched green as he was sick of seeing waste everywhere; a structural engineer who could not go home to his family in peace without addressing the huge environmental footprint for which he was responsible; a filmmaker, a computer programmer, several graphic artists, developers, architects... I always gave each person at least a half hour of my time (and sometimes considerably more) – time to listen and hear them out, and I have continued to meet with some on and off for the last few years.

Each conversation seemed to come back to the fact that people viewed green building as one of the rare focal points where significant change is possible and real solutions are being pursued. It seemed to these people the only place where their energies seemed to make sense even if they had absolutely no prior connection to the building industry. Some of them were quite baffled by it, but nonetheless convinced that being a part of the sustainability movement was essential to their personal growth. One thing I did figure out early on was that green building seemed to provide a sense of hope amidst this feeling of unease – a tangible feeling that it was an active part of solving the problem.

The problem with traditional environmental messaging, including Al Gore's movie, is that it focuses almost exclusively on the problems we are facing and does very little to address real solutions that go deeper than people driving a Prius and recycling. It is only when the credits roll in "An Inconvenient Truth" that solutions are even discussed, leaving many people with a feeling of despair and little direction. Guilt and despair are very poor motivators for long-term change – people need to know what to do. Green building provides an alternative, as it is a path toward significant change and a method by which people can make a meaningful contribution addressing climate change and other significant environmental problems. It deals with the problems at the source — how we live and work and the consumptive and wasteful buildings and communities that are the framework for our lives.

Green building allows individuals to become **agents of hope** within their communities (to borrow a phrase I first heard in a speech by the Premier of British Columbia) rather than mere harbingers of doom and gloom.

As this phenomenon seemed to grow I began to talk to other leaders in the green building and environmental fields and they shared some similar stories.

Something was beginning to change.

ZUGUNRUHE

While writing this book, I had the opportunity to talk with Janine Benyus, author of the best-selling *Biomimicry* about what I was witnessing. And because she was a biologist, I related to her what I was seeing in biological terms. I brought up the story of the hummingbird and other migratory animals and mentioned that the behavior I was witnessing was not unlike that of this bird or other migratory animals right before migration.

I explained how these people who were approaching me, for whatever reason, were picking up signals from the environment that change is coming and were compelled to change their way of life and their careers.

Always the teacher, Janine stepped in and said, "You know, there is a name for that." She proceeded to tell me about a concept called **zugunruhe**. Zugunruhe, a German word (pronounced zoo gen ROO ha), literally means "migratory restlessness" and is the definition encapsulating this known phenomenon of marked behavioral changes observed in many species prior to migration. Animals entering Zugunruhe indeed do become agitated and alter their eating habits, as well as other patterns such as mating and sleeping — leading up to their big journey. She told me she had witnessed similar changes, and we agreed that what it could be was the beginnings of our own cultural **Zugunruhe.** Such changes always begin with those who are most attuned and environmentally aware.

People like you.

As far as I am concerned, Zugunruhe should become a new word in our lexicon to describe all of us who seek to transform the way we live; restless for a new society that reconciles its relationship with the natural world.

Once people awaken to the magnitude of the issues that we face, many desire to become part of the solution in some way, since it is not possible to "go back to sleep" once you embrace the reality of these issues. It is this motivation, fueled by a growing awareness that change is coming (whether people are ready or not) that drove many of these individuals to seek me out when they did, since Cascadia is involved in some of the most far-reaching tools for change in the building industry today, perhaps best exemplified by the Living Building Challenge™ (that I will be discussing later in this book).

We cannot overstate the challenges that we face. The scientific community has been telling us for some time that unless we take drastic efforts to lower our environmental footprint and, in particular, cut our carbon emissions, our future as a species is in great danger. The health of all natural systems is not only declining, but the rate of that decline is increasing, made worse by the millions of humans that are added to the planet each year and the millions more appropriately yearning for higher living standards and unwittingly further reducing the planet's carrying capacity.

Scientists have known for several decades that we are responsible for climate change, but most have been surprised by the actual rate of change, which is showing disturbingly quickening trends. The website, architecture 2030.org, founded by architect Ed Mazria, has shown us what will happen to many of our coastal cities with only modest sea level rises predicted this century in most climate models. One need only think of the economic and cultural upheaval created by Hurricane Katrina in New Orleans to imagine what it would be like if every coastal city across the globe were affected.

The Katrina Diaspora that shook the United States becomes a global coastal Diaspora where every nation is affected.

We can now also readily see the beginning ripples of another disturbing interrelated trend – peak oil. At some point early in this decade, humanity crossed a threshold where more oil has been used than what remains in the ground, with each barrel becoming more expensive and difficult to extract. With prices rising, we are seeing only the beginnings of what will happen to an economy predicated on the availability of cheap oil. Looking at the rapidly increasing price of food also helps us to understand this interconnectedness and to forecast what might happen when gasoline prices reach six, eight, or twelve dollars a gallon.

TRANSFORMATION

What is needed is a complete transformation of our communities and the buildings and infrastructure within them for us to be truly sustainable – we desperately need a world filled with what I call Living Buildings and Living Communities[5].

While sounding far fetched only a few years ago, it is now entirely possible to reduce energy use within every single one of our communities by 60 to 80 percent within our lifetime with off-the-shelf technologies and knowledge that exists today. With such significant reductions in energy demand, it is also possible to make a complete switch to renewable energy (solar and wind) for the remaining energy we require. The world we seek could become the significant work of our generation, if only there were sufficient political and business will to do so – if only enough people awoke and began their own Zugunruhe.

Recently, the City of Juneau, Alaska was presented with a crisis that proves these points. It is a story that should have made front-page news all over the world, yet because nobody was killed and the story lacked cheap sensationalism, it barely got mentioned around the country.

In April 2008, a large avalanche occurred on the mountains outside of Juneau. The slide knocked out the city's main transmission lines and everyone lost power. Being prepared, Juneau switched the whole town over to diesel power and got service restored almost immediately. The problem was that the price of energy skyrocketed – from about

[5] International Living Building Institute www.ilbi.org

10 cents/kilowatt hour to 55 cents/kilowatt hour overnight. A 500 percent increase in people's bills. Many people suddenly could not pay their bills and the whole town of 30,000 people was faced with a real dilemma. What happened next was a powerful sociological study and a lesson in human behavior and incentives. Almost immediately the town saw a run on clothespins, followed by compact fluorescents and home energy monitors. People began unplugging appliances they were not using, shutting off their lights more diligently, figuring out when non-essential services really needed to be on, and etcetera. Within two weeks the town had cut its energy use by 35 percent — all from minor, painless steps that cost almost nothing. With real effort and intelligent investment, what is possible is easily double that.[6]

GREEN WARRIORS WELCOME

To move to a truly sustainable future, significant technical resources and knowledge must obviously be brought to bear. However, what are missing, I believe, are resources that teach us how to change as individuals. What do people do when they realize that they need to become an integral part of the solution? What tools are there for people caught up in the beginning stages of their own personal Zugunruhe?

How do they change their preconceptions about what is possible? How do they now react and interact with others not yet awake to the currently realities? How do they begin to challenge their own internal mythologies and "baggage"? The most fundamental obstacles to transformation are never technological or financial – but attitudinal and barriers of our own making. Zugunruhe does not instantly translate into profound personal enlightenment!

---

[6] Juneau has since got its power restored and while energy use has increased, the overall trend is somewhat positive – people are using slightly less energy and thinking about it much differently now.

Deep technological know-how gets you nowhere if you do not know how to collaborate and communicate. Profound change requires deep personal effectiveness that is not taught in our schools or is rarely discussed in the environmental and green building movements. We all struggle internally in ways that make us less effective than we could be.

Change is hard, and it is always much easier to tell someone else what to do differently than it is to coach ourselves when it is our own behavior that is limiting success – it is something that I remind myself as I write this book.

And yet I know I have been lucky to have had some incredible mentors who have indeed shared with me some powerful lessons in personal change. Lessons that have shaped and guided my own work within the sustainability movement. I now, through this book, humbly offer them to you – the reader – in the hopes that they will be as useful to you in your own Zugunruhe as they have been in mine.

Each chapter of this book is a separate essay, yet with a common thread that binds each together. I encourage you to read this book slowly – despite your restlessness for change – and to ponder and reflect on how you can become the most effective contributor to the change that lies ahead of us.

For like me, you can sense a migration….

And it is time to get ready

Welcome to **Zugunruhe.**

– Jason F. McLennan

01

GETTING YOUR OWN HOUSE IN ORDER

"When despair for the world grows in me, and I wake in the night at the least sound in fear of what my life and my children's lives may be – I go and lie down where the wood drake rests in his beauty on the water, and the great heron feeds. I come into the peace of wild things who do not tax their lives with forethought or grief. I come into the presence of still water. And I feel above me the day-blind stars waiting with their light. For a time I rest in the grace of the world, and am free."

—WENDELL BERRY

The root of the word eco is derived from the Greek (oikos) meaning "house" or "dwelling."

Any journey of consequence should begin by getting your own house in order. It is hard to attempt external change and to help others if you have not internalized the change and begun to live it. Zugunruhe produces an energy that should first be turned inward before it manifests outward. These steps are necessary for an authentic transformation.

That is not to say that you have to be an "eco-saint" and live a perfect green lifestyle before you begin your own migration. Quite the contrary. What matters most is that you begin and with each step forward, eyes are wide-open about the work that has yet to be done and the work that has in turn been done.

This book is not about guilt.

Any movement that requires all of its people to be saints is doomed. Instead, the ideas presented here are intended to help us recognize and accept our own imperfection as we go forward; to accept that we are complex beings with the capacity for foolishness even when at our best.

In real life, we have to compromise, reconciling our indulgences and contradictions as we strive for significant change. And the best place to begin such a journey is the place we are theoretically most comfortable and secure – our own house. Where better to practice and live the change we seek?

A transformed world does require transformed lifestyles and houses. And thankfully there are now a multitude of books that can tell you how to green your house and your lifestyle.

This book is not one of them.[1]

Rather than external things, Zugunruhe focuses on the internal transformation, although both are important. The person who exercises yet does not eat well still opens himself up to sickness, as does the person who takes perfect care of her body yet lives a life of stress and worry. Regardless of how modest or lavish it is, our "house" is both a physical manifestation and a metaphor of who we are. So begin to manifest the change you seek in society in your house and lifestyle today.

You do not have to be rich and have ample resources to reduce your own carbon footprint and ecological impact. It does require questioning your decisions and perhaps changing some important aspects of how you live your life, but these changes are usually for the better. Good decisions have nested results: less waste, more personal time, lower costs and lower environmental impact.

There is another reason to start in your house. As you begin your more fundamental journey – your personal zugunruhe to "be the change you wish to see in the world"– the people you hope to eventually influence will look for signs of insincerity. Be upfront about what you yourself are changing and what you continue to struggle with.

Be open, honest and real.

This approach, in and of itself, will bring about a form of change from the people you know. Ideas without sincerity rarely go far. Knowing that you are not a perfect eco-saint (admit it – you are not!) but that you are step-by-step lowering your environmental footprint can inspire much more deeply.

---

[1] The back of the book contains a suggested reading list including some resources to green your house and lifestyle.

People often ask me how I live my own ideals and bring the message home to my family and my life. What follows are some of the ways I do just that. I am far from perfect, and have much that I need to improve upon, but my family is always working on self-improvement in ways that lower our environmental footprint while enriching our lives.

MY LIFE

I have been blessed with a truly wonderful family. I married a beautiful, sensitive woman who is also my best friend. Tracy has a ton of patience and understanding – often more than I deserve. She is the glue that keeps our family together and moving forward, as I am often (too frequently) pulled in many directions with my work and environmental advocacy. Together, she and I have four children as part of a blended family. When I met Tracy, she had a great little three-year old named Julian. As a five-year-old, Julian stood with us at the altar in front of two hundred guests as the three of us each made vows to each other as part of a new family. As of this writing, that little boy is now a teenager who, as teenagers are programmed to do, keeps us on our toes.

Two years later, when Julian was seven, we welcomed Declan, my first biological child and an inquisitive little boy into our family. Declan loves to organize and design elaborate structures (like his dad) and seems to like books and ideas more than anything (also like his dad). When Declan was two, we had little Aidan, who is now a very scrappy little boy who does everything he can to keep up with his older brothers. Strong willed, headstrong, fearless and loving, Aidan seems to be one part warrior and one part cuddler – always willing to dive right into something and to come out swinging if needed.

Three boys! What a house we have. It is almost always chaos. They are loud, messy and full of life. Some days, it drives us absolutely crazy.

But we love it.

And we thought we were done!

But, sometimes life has a way of giving you what you want. In 2008, Rowan, our first girl (and last child!) was born. Rowan is so new we do not know what to expect from her, but we can already tell that she is much more reasonable than her brothers ever were. She almost always seems happy and is much more content – for now anyway. She will have a hard time finding a boyfriend when she is older, given how protective her three big brothers are of her. Even little Aidan – who is supposed to be jealous at his age wants nothing more than to comfort her and snuggle with her. She has an inner joy for life that makes all of us simply smile.

One thing is certain: it is easier to live an ecological life when you are single. When you only have yourself to account for, you have complete control. As you grow a family, "control" takes on a different meaning. You learn compromise, you teach as best you can, you lead by example and sometimes things are not easy. Life changes what you do. Bringing children into the world is a magical thing – and it is a huge commitment to the planet. There are now seven billion of us (just about) and we are a hungry, demanding species that takes more than its share.

Each of us potentially adds a significant burden to an already stretched global ecosystem. Tracy and I are cognizant of this reality, having a larger-than-average family for this country – the most wasteful in the world. As a result, we work hard to make sure that the footprint of our family does not follow the pattern of a typical North American household. We teach our children to be responsible stewards, to love and respect nature, to conserve and respect resources and to do simple things like turn off the faucet and turn off the lights (and the ever present battle with the teenager to take short showers). Ultimately, though, we know that the majority of their environmental impact will be up to them and to their choices...their own zugunruhe. As much as we wish it – it will be up to them to find their own path and knowledge of the challenges that they will face.

Like any parent, I secretly wish great things for my children. We can not help wanting to live vicariously through them in some regard and project our own desires onto them. I am not immune and have silly dreams for my children. For example, I really want one of them to be a professional tennis player and I want to go along to the French Open and Wimbledon. But another wish is more profound:

I hope that they truly do become part of the solution – and part of the generation that got us back on track – as a civilization sustainably integrated into the web of life.

HOME

I live in one of the strangest houses you could imagine. It is a cross between a tree house, a lighthouse and a yacht. In fact, before the original designer drew up his plans for the house, he lived on a yacht and wanted this structure to be a natural extension of the lifestyle to which he became accustomed. The resulting "land-yacht" contains about 2800 square feet[2] – but spread out on five levels! (It is reminiscent of the Once-ler's house in Dr. Suess's *The Lorax*.) For a house with six people in it, it is not overly big by American standards. But there are lots of stairs, great character and great views.

From an environmental standpoint, there are several interesting things about the house. It was constructed in the 1970s almost

---

[2] Which, on a square foot/person basis, is considerably lower than the national average.

completely out of salvaged rather than new building materials. The designer, a local architect by the name of Bill Isley, got all of the wood from an old industrial warehouse that was torn down in Tacoma. The wood was barged across the sound and giant 3x12s were used to frame the house around a center core of four giant re-used telephone poles[3]. Other salvaged materials included doors, windows, hardware and lighting fixtures. From an embodied energy and resource conservation standpoint, it is almost impossible to beat.

The site design is also unique. The house was sensitively sited and nestled within the trees with minimal site-disturbance and a footprint that is quite small (aided by its tower-like structure) for a house its size. The house was part of a unique development of six homes, all intricately placed within a healthy second-growth forest using a common shared gravel drive for minimum site disturbance and water run-off. The building operates within a healthy water balance (water comes from an on-site spring and ends up being re-charged on-site) and because the majority of the site is left in a natural state with almost no impervious surfaces, rainfall is given a chance to recharge the aquifer. There are no "lawns" or artificial landscape in the development.

Unfortunately, when we moved in, the house was not as energy efficient as I would have liked. Many of the salvaged windows were single pane[4], and the original mechanical systems from the 1970s were still intact and in use. So the first thing I did was to replace all the lighting with compact fluorescent bulbs and I insulated the crawlspace. Then I replaced the heating system with an efficient air-source heat pump and replaced the hot water heater. I programmed our thermostat with aggressive night setback temperatures and with a wider comfort zone criteria than typical, since we have found that we can be comfortable in the winter at 68F instead of 72F. Finally, I had a blower door test done and I began the process of caulking and

---

[3] Thankfully not dipped in creasote.

[4] The house has a weird mixture of single and double pane windows – apparently depending upon what he could find salvaged.

sealing the building to control infiltration. Energy use is now down by 40 per cent since I moved in with more infiltration work still to be done. I have also installed dual flush toilets-significantly cutting water use as well.

As I can afford to, I will replace windows which are currently holding further performance gains back. My goal is to cut energy use another 10 to 20 percent over the next couple of years. All of that said, I recognize that I do live in a single-family residence, and that while much easier to raise kids in, it is not as easy on the environment as I would like it to be as compared to a more dense urban housing type.

But it is part of the overall picture... let's move on to food!

FOOD

Food is a big deal in our family. We like good food and pay careful attention to it. I personally find cooking to be relaxing and rewarding, and I take extra satisfaction in knowing where my food comes from and how it was raised. As a result, we eat locally and buy seasonally. We belong to a community-supported agriculture (CSA) program, where we share in the risks and rewards with a local farmer. Each week for almost half of the year, our farmer delivers us a box filled with wonderful organic surprises, all grown within fifty miles of our door. Having to use what you get inspires creative cooking. (Sometimes you even get more than what you need; this year was a bumper crop in cucumbers, which inspired us to make our own pickles.) Experimentation has expanded our palettes and our culinary possibilities in wonderful ways. Best of all, since the CSA program reduces the trips to the grocery story (where you often buy stuff you do not really need), it is affordable as well. Nothing tastes as good as really fresh vegetables that have not sat on a truck or shelf for a week.

Have you ever tried home-made tomato soup with ingredients from local fresh produce and compared it to the canned stuff? Wow.

I supplement these vegetables in the summer months with other produce from our local farmers' market, where I always stock up on my favorite things such as potatoes, arugula, spring onions and beets.

I am increasingly growing more of our own food. (Above is a picture of one of my containers where I grow herbs for cooking and a few extra vegetables).

Tracy and I enjoy teaching our children how to grow food and to see the direct connection between planting, growth, harvesting and eating. It is amazing how excited a five-year-old can get when he eats a small carrot he planted himself a couple of months earlier. Eating seasonally also brings you closer in touch with the cycles of nature and I believe enriches the eating experience. Asparagus should only be eaten for about a month – then one should move on and savor the next crop. And slathering butter onto a new potato just out of the ground is a heavenly experience. I am admittedly a poor farmer – (having grown up in a mining town with acidified soil, it is not exactly in my blood). But I am learning and enjoying the process immensely.

When I was in college, I made a conscious choice to give up red meat in order to lower the footprint of my eating habits. I have not had a hamburger or steak or lambchop since. My family now shares this habit (except the teenager who rebels by eating beef whenever he can); we only eat local free-range chicken and fish that comes from well-managed fisheries on the Pacific Coast where we live. As much as possible, our food does not come from outside the West Coast or from more than a few hundred miles away. (Exceptions include olive oil, orange juice, chocolate and coffee –okay and some cereal and kid snacks too.) Our wine, beer and other items are primarily local. I even bake a good portion of

the bread we eat, which adds to homemade pies, bagels, and other confections that I learned to make from my mother and grandmother. Food that has not spent a great deal of time on a truck is not only better for the planet but also for the palate. It is hard to compare fresh-baked artisan bread with anything wrapped in plastic in a grocery story.

These are a couple of my chickens; we have quite a few now, and since my kids get to name them they have names like: Dragon, Black Rhino, White Chocolate and the Destroyer. Their real lives and behavior are not so dramatic. We raised each of them from chicks, and they now provide our family with fresh eggs every morning. We do not live on a farm, but I house them in a great little pen that is designed to keep out just about everything that tries to eat them… (do not ask me about racoons and the great chicken genocide we had). Exposing my children to domesticated animals and the responsibility to raise them has been an incredible experience. I personally think everyone should have chickens.

TRANSPORTATION

How you get around in life has a great deal to do with your environmental footprint. Where you live, where you work and the locations of your essential services work together to lock you into a certain level of impact (which we will explore a bit more later in the book). For my part, I have become quite intentional about my own transportation footprint even while living in a single-family home.

A typical work week has me working from home two or three days a week, with no transportation required. My wife works from home every day. The rise in telecommuting has significant potential for reducing societal environmental burdens. It also leaves more time for family. On days I work from home, I can walk my son to the bus stop, have lunch with my three-year old and personally make dinner for my family since I am not losing time on the road. The typical downside is the lack of collaboration. In my case, I collaborate personally with colleagues on the days when I go to the office. On those days, I take the bus to the ferry terminal and then walk to work on the other side[5]. No car is needed or wanted for most trips. When I do have to drive somewhere, I drive a Smartcar that gets 45 miles per gallon on the highway when I drive it responsibly and not too fast. I also have a Corbin Sparrow electric car, which is very cool and has an even lower footprint but is simply not as reliable.

Airline travel is my Achilles heel. Like many in the green building movement, I fly too much. I get asked to do a lot of speeches, and even though Cascadia offsets our carbon impacts, it is a burden I wish I could discard. I rationalize that I am doing more good than harm by promoting green building in all the places I visit.

Let's hope I am right about that.

---

[5] I live on Bainbridge Island.

STUFF

No matter how hard you try, there always seems to be too much "stuff". Children in particular seem to attract stuff like magnets. For my family's part, we try to engage in a cycle of reuse by getting as much as we can from consignment shops (easier for the little ones, but harder for the self-conscious older ones) and we recycle and compost to keep "wasted" stuff to a minimum. Our weekly trash is quite small for a family our size. Regardless, stuff creeps in.

When I was single, I was quite proud that I did not own a TV. For years I kept TV completely out of my life. I watched movies on my computer, but otherwise stuck to reading. Now we have three TVs! I fought cable for two years but then lost that battle too. More than ever, there is huge pressure to consume. Children are barraged with ads and peer pressure to have things. We are all part of a culture that rewards the collection of stuff, and frankly there are a lot of cool things out there to want. There is even an explosion of so-called "eco-friendly" goods (although with questionable true environmental value).

I have met a few (but not many) families that lead a more "pure" life when it comes to stuff, but we know we are doing the best we can. We are very careful about where we spend our money, where products come from, how energy efficient our possessions are, whether or not they use energy and how much waste is created as a result of our purchases. It is hard at times, but each year I think we continue to do better.

These are just some aspects of my life and details on my own attempts to improve my standing as a citizen of the planet. I hope this information triggers some thinking and action in yours. As I mentioned there are a ton of good books that can provide guidance in how to green your lifestyle and house. As we go forward, we leave the material realm behind. Most likely most of you have already begun the process of getting your house in order. And once your house is in order, it is time to begin the much harder work of inner transformation.

Let's Zugunruhe.

02

IN THE SHADOW OF GIANTS:
FINDING MENTORSHIP

"The Man who does not read good books has no advantage
over the man who can't read them."
—MARK TWAIN

"An expert is a man who has stopped thinking – he knows!"
—FRANK LLOYD WRIGHT

In almost all fields, there is a tendency for the media to create "stars" of people and to cast them in such a light as to imply that their creative achievements are born without compromise, without collaboration and without precedent. Pure creative talent as proof of the highest pinnacle of human creation is given. The environmental and sustainability fields are no exception.

It is a myth so many of us buy into; we assume that great contributions can only be made by "great people," and to be truly successful we must emulate the mythologies of these legends, working in isolation until our contributions are "ready." We seem to want heroes to worship, but in so doing we separate ourselves and our co-workers from the reality that we can all have impact.

As a designer, I have often found this to be a fascinating topic. Can we all affect profound change? Can we in fact work together as a movement to see great changes happen? Or, is creative genius achieved in isolation and "movements" always led by great leaders?

Do the "masters" draw solely from their own pure inspiration, uninfluenced by their predecessors and surroundings? Was Ayn Rand's fictional Howard Roark (a loosely interpreted caricature of Frank Lloyd Wright) an accurate personification of untouchable – and untouched – greatness?

I think not. In fact, I know not. To give a powerful example I turn to a world I know well – architecture.

In the architectural world, the current crop of "starchitects" includes such popular figures as Frank Gehry, Richard Rogers, Zaha Hadid and Rem Koolhaas. Magazines, books and documentaries present the work of these individuals as solo efforts, despite the fact that architecture, more than any art form, is a collaborative process involving many talented and dedicated individuals. The grander the facility, the more individuals required to work on it and the less overall control the lead individual typically has. Having been part of an office that worked with "starchitects" such as Steven Holl and Moshe Safdie, I know first-hand that "genius" is as much "collective" as it is "individual". When talented professionals work well together, they can produce incredible architecture. When they do not, buildings suffer greatly. Regardless, the "starchitect" system of hero worship results in the largest and most prominent architectural commissions going to a short list of a few dozen, almost all white, male designers. These notable commissions disproportionately influence trends in architecture and building, helping to define what is "cool" and acceptable to emulate while discounting and failing to mention the range of talents – the other architects, the engineers, the builders and the visionary clients that truly made the architecture great.

As it turns out, this isolated genius hero worship mythology has had significant environmental implications. Until very recently, few of the top architects openly promoted an environmental ethic in their building. Instead, they tended to reinforce the notion that their work should be "above" mere constraints such as energy conservation, indoor air quality and use of local materials. As a result, many of the most prominent and visited works of architecture around the world are actually environmentally irresponsible and use considerably more energy and resources than they should. Is this right? Should not large civic projects that are meant to define a city or region be required to operate efficiently and without polluting in addition to being beautiful and inspiring? When a star system pervades, fashion, rather than pragmatism and meaningful beauty can take hold. And if "green" is not currently cool – then fashion moves people away from responsible solutions.

As with the influence of Michael Jordan, Tiger Woods and Roger Federer in the sports world, top architects wield enormous influence in the building trades, architecture schools and within firms. New materials and systems are brought into fashion, details are made trendy and something that was designed to work in one climate or situation is copied in many disparate climates and situations. Until the "cool" architects all begin to care, a large percentage of the industry will be ambivalent to the challenges we face. A building that wins design awards yet makes people sick or uses three times the energy that it could use is not a good building. It is an irresponsible building – and should not be emulated carte blanche.

So what does this have to do with Zugunruhe? A couple of very important things, in fact.

1. HERO WORSHIP IS NOT THE SAME AS MENTORSHIP

As you begin to work on your own inner transformation it is critically important to find mentors. And people sometimes confuse hero worship with mentorship and look for one guru to help them with everything they need – or worse, they wait for some great leader to tell them what to do. The environmental movement and sustainability is a movement not of one great leader – but of an army of individuals working collaboratively together – which means that you have an integral role to play. Let's keep using architecture as our example:

The mythology of the lone genius goes against the fundamental tenets of green architecture and sustainability. If architecture is treated as pure art, then its creators can not be bothered by ecological concerns. Indeed, the earliest forms of green architecture were viewed by many as little more than a distraction that steered the focus away from great work. In actuality, the green movement has added meaning and complexity to the architectural practice unlike anything since the rise of building codes and the general awareness of public safety. By its very nature, it requires acknowledging that a truly successful building is a partnership between many disciplines practicing an integrated design approach.

2. IT TAKES MULTIPLE MENTORS

As you prepare for your journey and you do, in fact, begin to look for mentors, you will find that you need many of them. Sustainability is a rich, diverse field and, as with ecosystem health, the greater diversity the more robust and resilient the solutions you will come up with. In architecture, the most successful projects are designed and built by integrating a variety of ideas, and by responding to ecology, place, climate and culture which is always complex, messy and specific. Nature – not ego and fashion – dictates the parameters of a green building. Industry giants and their contributions are by no means rejected; they are simply factored into the larger whole of influences.

3. EVERY MENTOR IN TURN HAS A MENTOR

Find a great idea and dig deep enough and behind it is another idea. Find a great mentor and behind them are several others. It is a thrilling thing to realize as you reach out to find new mentors that you are merely part of a continuum of mentorship and teaching that stretches behind and will stretch into the future. Any great leader is a product of good mentorship and for you to have the impact you desire you will first need to learn from others.

As much as some of the most celebrated architects have enjoyed taking exclusive credit for their work, they all have had predecessors and, yes, even mentors. Frank Lloyd Wright himself, famously self-congratulatory, relied on the influence of Louis Sullivan but only rarely admitted it. And when it came to other contemporaries that most likely did influence his work, they were simply never acknowledged. He no doubt had many teachers and mentors. If you think you are going to make great change or save the planet on your own, get over yourself now.

We all walk in the shadows of others and in turn cast our own shadows on the people we teach.

How wonderful it is to fully appreciate that the web of connections in life extends even to our own ideas – that at our most original we should be humbled and thankful for those who made having such an idea possible.

IN THE SHADOWS OF MY OWN GREEN GIANTS

The green architecture movement of which I am so closely connected is starting to produce its own "green stars," but if you talk to most of them, what I find quite fulfilling is that they will often speak quite freely about those who shaped their work and ideas – they are quick to attribute much of their success to others.

Sim Van der Ryn, an early leader in the green architecture movement and a former California State Architect, has never hesitated to laud those who have taught and influenced him throughout his life and career. When I was in college, I read an article he published, "The Patron Saints of Ecological Design," in which he focused not on his own achievements but on those of the mentors who paved his way. It was – and continues to be – important to Van der Ryn to acknowledge that he did not arrive at his place in the profession fully formed. His life experiences, combined with guidance and support provided by predecessors, helped make him an instrumental figure in the green movement.

I personally walk daily in the substantial shadows cast by my personal collection of mentors, each of whom has played a unique role in forming my personal and professional self. The fact that each of these individuals is careful to attribute their teachings to their own mentors helps them appear even greater in my eyes — not as mythology, but because they are willing to be approachable and real.

Bob Berkebile   Pliny Fisk III

From the time I first met him, when he served as my boss at Berkebile Nelson Immenschuh McDowell Architects (BNIM) in Kansas City, I knew that Bob Berkebile would have an enormous impact on my life as he has for many in our movement. Indeed, I soon thought of him more as a teacher than a supervisor, and I have no doubt that I will spend the rest of my days referring to him as my greatest professional mentor. Although he sat higher on the hierarchical professional ladder in the early days of our working relationship, he insisted that our collaboration was based more on sharing and growing together rather than on my implementing his ideas. His ability to inspire people to seek the best within themselves and their projects makes him who he is – and is how he leaves his sizeable mark. Bob is too humble to take credit for this skill; he insists that he simply continues in the footsteps of his builder father, his fellow partners at the firm, many of his clients and his own greatest mentor, Buckminster Fuller.

I consider Pliny Fisk, III another of my great teachers. Pliny's uncanny visionary scope, which I first observed while collaborating with him on a project in Montana, allows him to find the massive and minute connections within any system simultaneously. As a pioneer in the green building movement, he has taught many of us about how to take a much broader look at the challenges we face in order to find the most effective solutions. Because of this, Pliny is almost always ten years ahead of the movement's next step. When I expand my thinking and shoot for the big idea, it is Pliny's influence at work. Pliny, too, credits his own mentors for the wisdom he has gained in his life, speaking often of such greats as Ian McCarg and Louis Kahn, under whom he studied. He also credits what he has learned from his students and interns at the Center for Maximum Building Potential, which he co-directs with his equally visionary wife, Gail Vittori.

Ron Perkins, another pioneer with whom I was fortunate enough to collaborate while working at BNIM, taught me a great deal about logical problem solving and "cutting to the essence" of a situation. By watching him, I learned how to seek the underlying truth of any project, and how to overcome the inevitable barriers of any endeavor. When Ron speaks of his personal heroes, he refers to Lee Eng Lock and Amory Lovins, both individuals who have contributed deeply to the green building movement.

Even when we can not always access them personally, great mentors offer their wisdom through writings and seminars. I have been transformed by the writings of Paul Hawken (*The Ecology of Commerce*), Janine Benyus (*Biomimicry*) and John Ralston Saul (*Voltaire's Bastards*). My personal list of life-changing written works grows longer by the day, and I am on a never-ending quest to learn from the experiences others have had and have been generous enough to document.[1]

In the green building world, most know the story of Ray Anderson, the influential and successful CEO of Interface Carpets. Asked once to address the company's sales force and familiarize them with the company's environmental stance, he felt that simple legal compliance was not enough of a foundation on which to base corporate policy. So he began researching environmental issues, particularly touched by the messages in Hawken's book. When it came time to speak to his employees, he possessed a new and – for him – radically different understanding of the potential damage a company such as his could do to the planet. Beginning on that day, he challenged his people to follow him into a new era of corporate environmental responsibility. That was 1994, and Anderson still refers to it as his "conversion experience." Interface established a green goal of being fully sustainable by 2020, and continues on this journey today. By seeking a mentor even while himself a highly successful businessman, one man thereafter changed the face of an industry. Interface led a revolution in the carpet manufacturing industry to be more environmentally responsible, and the effects of his efforts will continue to ripple outwards for generations.

As a result, I believe that I owe the lion's share of my own successes to the mentors that I have had. Through watching and working with them, and most importantly by being open to what they had to teach and observing carefully not only what they said, but also how they said it, I have been

---

[1] The appendix of this book contains the second green warrior reading list – a sequel to the reading list found in my first book, *The Philosophy of Sustainable Design*, published in 2004.

able to grow my own effectiveness more quickly, which is where the first lesson (or Gwersi at the end of this chapter) of Zugunruhe comes into play.

CASTING YOUR OWN GREEN SHADOW

Finding mentors is only the first half of a continuum of learning that defines what I call a "green warrior".

To be effective, we must all be willing to be mentors as well; to teach as well as to be taught. Most people who are not professional educators find very little time to stop and teach someone, be it their co-workers, clients or even their own children. Many times people get so caught up in their own issues and tribulations that it simply does not occur to them to teach something to someone who is struggling with an issue that we have already tackled. At other times people simply assume that they have nothing to teach. Given our hero-worship culture that steeps us in feelings of inadequacy, people are either afraid to reach out or they simply can not imagine that their ideas would add anything of value. How sad and how wrong!

I learned this lesson with the help of a college classmate who offered up a piece of wisdom that I have carried with me ever since. While studying architecture at the University of Oregon, I began volunteering at the University Solar Information Center, a student-led organization created to disseminate information on solar energy and green design to the Eugene-Springfield community. The director at that time was Matthew Swett, a young and bright master's student in architecture. After only a month on the job, I fielded a call from a local citizens' group asking for help in their efforts to convince a building owner to install solar panels on his property. Since we were the "Solar Center," they hoped we could help out. I told Matthew about the opportunity, hoping that he would take care of it. Instead, he said, "Jason, they talked to you, why don't you lead this meeting?" I was taken aback – I was new! And just a student! "How can I help them?," I asked out loud. I was extremely concerned that my limited knowledge on the subject would reveal my inadequacies, and I quickly asked Matthew to reconsider sending me as the Center's ambassador.

In his quiet and calm way, Matthew said something to me that I have never forgotten. "It's important to remember, Jason: if you know one thing that someone else doesn't, you can teach it. Be upfront with what you don't know, but always be willing to share what you do." It was sage advice from a young man.

He proceeded to ask me all that I knew on the topic of solar panels. I drew from what I felt was a cursory understanding of photovoltaics and I told him what I knew. He kept asking me simple questions, and in a few minutes I had completed a mini-seminar on solar panels – their optimal design, placement, general sizing, major hurdles and barriers to implementation. I began to grin.

Matthew, observing my realization, reminded me that I actually had a lot to teach. He gave me the confidence first to rely on, then build on what I knew and not to feel shame about what I did not know. I ended up going to the meeting, presenting information the group found very helpful, and returning to the Solar Center feeling empowered by my knowledge as well as by my desire to seek wisdom from peers. I never again passed up an opportunity to share knowledge that I had already learned. Matthew, a classmate, took the time to teach me and it shifted the way I looked at my abilities to teach others.

As members of the green movement racing against the clock, we are all responsible for teaching others as we need to help people leapfrog to greater understanding as soon as possible. By being willing always to teach what we know, we play a critical role in creating the changes needed in the world. Regardless of where you are on your journey you have a dual role as mentor and mentee.

An Illuminating Example – Chuck Rusch

When I was a student at the University of Oregon, I met an architecture professor by the name of Charles "Chuck" Rusch. He was a quiet faculty member, with a decidedly low-key lecture style. Some students overlooked his lessons because he was not "flashy" or in your face like some. But I was intrigued by his presence and decided to look deeper into what Chuck had to say and that turned out to be one of the best decisions I ever made during my academic career.

Chuck was what author Daniel Quinn calls a "maieutic" teacher (from the root maia, meaning midwife), as he was one who acts as a midwife to pupils, gently guiding their own understanding so that their answers come from within. He delivered a much deeper and lasting style of teaching than what was traditionally taught. Since many students these days have become accustomed to someone merely telling them what to think, Chuck appeared too subtle for some.

But buried within Rusch's soft delivery were pearls of wisdom; perhaps more than any I had received from professors I had met up to that time. It just took a bit of "active listening" to hear those pearls. With Chuck, learning was a two-way process. After the first class, I was so touched that I looked for other opportunities to study with him. In my final year, we began meeting weekly on an informal basis to discuss books, philosophy, design, sustainability, the past and the future. I was lucky enough to experience the substance of this man, whom some had overlooked.

What I found out was that I was the newest member of a large group of young people who benefited from Rusch's unique teaching skills. Years before, during his tenure at UCLA, where he taught prior to his appointment at Oregon, Rusch became disillusioned with the quality of education his children were receiving in the schools they attended. He told me of the day his son came home from school crying because his teacher was making him study a book he had already read the previous summer. Instead of allowing him to pick another book, the teacher told him that he had to stick to the curriculum and not to worry because it would mean that the course would be easier for him! But what about learning? He saw the lights going out in his children's eyes and felt compelled to do something.

So he did the unusual. He took a sabbatical from teaching architecture to college students and started a new school where he would teach his own children and others from the community whose parents were also dissatisfied with the school system. Chuck had no training in teaching younger children, nor a school in which to teach them. But what he started was a remarkable experiment in learning. The school became known as Moboc for "Mobile Open Classroom." It had no building, desks or established curriculum. Instead, Rusch relied on the city's surroundings as inspiration for lessons, and on the students' innate desire to learn as motivation for their education. He realized that the city was filled with parks, libraries, museums and other facilities that were never used during the day. So, instead of keeping chilren within the same confined space, he brought them to the experience. The school was transformative and his children – and a majority of the children who went on to attend his mobile school – excelled.

Chuck made everyone in the community a mentor, calling on people in factories, shops and offices to give time to these students, enriching their lives in the process and often being taught themselves through the quality of the children's questions. Chuck also used the students to teach each other, understanding that by teaching they were greatly reinforcing their own understanding. Chuck himself was often humbled by the depth of their insight.

On one memorable day in a Los Angeles park, Rusch guided the students in a lesson in mathematics that started with a simple exercise in tree identification. Here is the story in Chuck's own words:

On the first day of school, we had lunch in one of the Los Angeles city parks. After lunch I gathered everyone and I said, "Let's do some tree identification." And they all moaned. So I said, "Aw, come on. You live with these plants, you could at least know their names. What's the name of these trees we're sitting under?"

They all looked up and in unison said, "Sycamores." So I said, "What kind of sycamore?" And no one knew. I got out my Trees of North America book and said, "Let's find out." There were only three kinds of sycamores in the book. Only one on the West Coast, and it was called the California Sycamore. I thought it was all over, but I persisted. "We'd better make sure by checking these trees against the description in the book." So I started reading the text. Leaves 6-8 inches. I fished a cloth measuring tape out of a box, handed it to Jeff and said, "Go check out those leaves." He found that the leaves were indeed 6-8 inches.

I went back to the book and read. Height of mature trees, 30-50 feet. How are we going to check that? A big discussion followed, and we finally decided that I should stand up against one of the trees, they would back off as far as they could and estimate how many Rusches' height the tree was. A little simple multiplication followed and we had an approximate tree height. Everyone was pretty involved by now, so I asked them. "How else could you do it?" Eric was in the seventh grade and knew a little geometry. So he taught us how to measure the height by triangulation.

I was delighted just to have everyone's attention, so I went back to the book and kept reading. Near the bottom of the paragraph came the clincher. Diameter 1-3 feet. So I handed over the measuring tape and said, get me the diameter of that tree over there. They went over to the tree, and it wasn't until they were right on top of it that they realized that the only way to measure the diameter of tree directly is to cut it down. But I insisted that we had to know the diameter of the tree, so two of them stretched out the tape next to the tree, and by eyeballing along one edge and then the other, they came up with 18 inches. I said, " Is that an accurate answer or just approximate?" They agreed it was only a guess, so I said," how else could you do it?"

Right off Daniel said, "Well you could measure all the way around it, lay that circle out in the dirt, and then measure across it. I was *really impressed and said, "Go to it!" Meanwhile, I turned to the rest of the group and said, "How else could you do it?"*

Eric, who turned out to be a visualizer and was perhaps visualizing the tree as having two sides said, "Well, you could measure all the way around it. And divide by two." Since I believe you learn at least as much from mistakes as from successes, I said, "Okay, try it." Meanwhile, Daniel was measuring across the circle on the ground, and by picking the right points on a somewhat lopsided circle came up with the same answer of 18 inches. So I gave the tape to Eric, he measured around the tree, got 60 inches, divided by 2 and got 30 for a diameter. He was naturally a little disappointed, so I said:

"Well, I like your idea. Maybe you just have the wrong number. Is there a better number to divide by than two?" Right away, Michael said, "Well you could divide by 3," and then thinking ahead added, "And subtract 2." I said, "Great! Now you have a formula: check it out on that tree over there," pointing to one only about 6 inches in diameter. They went over, measured the circumference, divided by 3, subtracted 2 and checked it against a circle on the ground. The result was disappointing. So I told them to try some more trees. They checked about three more trees and came back. How did it work?

"Well," Mark said. "Dividing by 3 works pretty well but subtracting isn't so good."

"How good is dividing by 3?" I asked, and Michael replied, "It's not quite big enough."

"How big should it be?"

"About 3 ½," said Daniel. "No!" said Michael. "It's more like 3 1/8."

At that point, these five kids, ranging in age from 9 to 12, were within 2 one-hundredths of discovering pi and I was having trouble containing myself. I suppose I could have extended the lesson by having them convert 1/8 into decimals, but I was too excited.

"Look," I said. "I want to tell you a secret. There's a magic number, which is so special it has its own name. It's called pi. And the magic is that once you know how big it is, you can take any circle, no matter or how big or small, and go from circumference to diameter or diameter to circumference. Now here's how it works...."

Chuck later related, "I know that I didn't really understand pi until I got into college, despite an excellent math program in high school. But for those five kids at least, pi is something real. It lives in trees and telephone poles."

Rusch believed that Moboc was successful because it was based on the notion of "found learning" – the spontaneous, effortless process of learning we all experience naturally. When we are forced to gain knowledge, Rusch said, we are resistant to it. When we perceive the material to be relevant to our lives, we are more open to it. The children who experienced this vision first-hand continue to stand in the long, strong shadow of Chuck Rusch...and he in theirs.

As you begin your Zugunruhe I encourage you to find your Chuck Rusch and reconnect with those whose shadows you walk in.

GWERSI I

Find a mentor, not a hero.

In fact, seek many.

We all walk in the shadows of others and must begin by acknowledging and honoring those who have taught us.

To be effective, one must continually search for mentorship

Regardless of age or years of experience.

Be humble and learn from those who teach you.

GWERSI II

If you know one thing, teach that.

All of us should see teaching others as part of our own growth

As it brings clarity and coherence to one's own understanding

While lifting up and advancing others.

It is a gift of spirit and a chance to test ideas.

Anyone can be a teacher with immense value.

It only requires knowing just one thing that someone else does not.

Be brave and confident,

For your insights have value and beauty.

THE ASCENDANCY OF THE POLYMATH:
CHARTING A COURSE TO THE INFORMED GENERALIST

"Diversity confers resilience, adaptability and the
capacity for regeneration."
—JANINE BENYUS

Experts help make the world go 'round. Of this, there is no dispute. Individuals who are extremely knowledgeable about specific subjects and are able to weave their particular expertise into a broader framework bring great value to any undertaking. This is as true in medicine, science and the arts as it is in green building and environmental fields.

Since World War II, however, and especially since the 1980s, there has been a gradual shift in the balance between generalization and specialization. We are now living amid an abundance of specialized experts – those who focus only on small segments of their chosen fields and feel less of a connection to the larger contexts in which they operate. The success of a scientific reductionist philosophy taught and preached for decades has become ingrained in our definition of an expert or knowledgeable individual; someone without a Ph.D. is deemed irrelevant and incapable to provide expert commentary. In fact, as a society we continue to devalue education that produces a more well-rounded person. We are too quick to reduce funding for the arts and humanities in favor of more "practical" fields such as mathematics, business or science. Is one truly more valuable than the other? Or do the arts and humanities in fact provide a much needed balance?

When you bring this over-specialized approach to the design and construction of a building or a community design, the result can be a loss of understanding of the whole. Experts deal exclusively with their own focal area of a project rather than taking a step back to consider the overall goals of the endeavor or issues outside of their scope of learning. I strongly believe that such a piecemeal process is not only bad for a single building, but it can be catastrophic for the environment at large.

And yet, our whole educational system, including those programs that prepare people for the environmental fields, promotes the idea of the specialist as the highest achievement of education. Should someone in a state of zugunruhe who wants to make a greater difference by changing the built environment return to school to get more and more specialized degrees and follow the cultural norms? Or should we embrace a new, broader-based system of expert development to tackle the challenges we currently face? While it is certainly useful to have a deep seated expertise, it is perhaps time to look differently at how we prepare and educate ourselves for the future.

TURNING TO THE GENERALIST

There is absolutely no need...to turn out 21 year old specialists equipped with no memory of their civilization's experience, no ethical context, no sense of the larger shape of their society.
—John Ralston Saul

In a climate of specialization, we need to recognize the value of the generalist – the polymath – who is educated, informed and experienced in multiple disciplines. The polymath is qualified to look at the overriding goals and realities of a problem and guide the decision-making process accordingly to the ultimate benefit of the project as well as the planet. This approach is especially important when realizing that the nature of the problems we now face were created exactly because a reductionist, isolated approach was used. Ironically, our society, when confronted with highly complex systems such as ecosystems and planetary health, ignores the complexity and begins by studying things in pieces rather than as systems.

Take a typical building for example (which is much less complex than even the simplest ecosystem). Realistically, anything larger than a house requires the expertise of a number of specialists. That will never change. Construction methodologies have become extremely complicated, and no individual could possibly retain the level of expertise required to understand all phases and components of any one project. The problem is that in most building design processes, there is little communication and true collaboration between each specialist. The results are buildings that waste considerable energy and resources as synergies are not properly explored. Specialists should never be allowed to practice in isolation as significant leaps in performance are only possible when silos are broken and synergies between systems designed by specialists are exploited.

It is the generalist who needs to captain the ship as only he or she can understand enough of the whole to bring coherence, order, beauty and efficiency to bear. In many ways, the architect is the last great generalist profession. The architect knows less about any individual component of a building than the specialist engineer or builder, yet knows considerably more about the whole. The architecture profession has changed significantly in recent times as well. More and more architects are being funneled into a specialist mode of training and career development – working time and again on the same building types and playing their own version of the isolated expert. In these specialist situations, it becomes highly valuable to add individuals to a team who completely broaden the nature of the dialogue. For example, large-scale projects that have great civic impact should include artists and biologists at the table yet still be captained by a generalist who has an appreciation of both art and science.

It is the skills of the synthesizer, of the individual who can see the whole picture, that is most needed in this current paradigm to make the scale of changes necessary. And I predict that in a complete reversal from the last few decades, it is the generalist who will be in greater demand and of greater use to society in the coming decades as we attempt to solve many of the most challenging environmental problems that are beginning to plague us.

LEARNING FROM BAD EXAMPLES

To find proof of the potentially drastic effects of over-specialization, one need only look at a handful of examples from recent environmental history.

- Twenty years after the introduction of DDT, which earned its discoverer a Nobel Prize, biologist Rachel Carson proved the pesticide's catastrophic effects on human health and the environment. Dozens of scientists highly specialized in chemistry touted the safety and benign qualities of the chemical. It took biologists and "generalist" environmentalists to prove them wrong.

- MBT, a rubber additive widely used in a number of industrial applications, has now been shown to have extremely toxic and long-lasting ecological and bio-chemical effects when it too was deemed "completely safe" for use. Unfortunately it continues to be used.

- Decades after CCA-treated lumber was heralded as the ideal material to use in gardens, picnic tables and children's climbing structures, we now know that the embedded chemicals – including inorganic arsenic – actually seep readily from the lumber and could easily poison our children and ourselves. It took people like my friend Bill Walsh, an attorney leading the Healthy Building Network, to bring an end to CCA lumber sales.

- Chlorofluorocarbons (CFCs) were invented by Thomas Midgley, the man also responsible for introducing the world to leaded gasoline. Midgley won a Nobel Prize for his discoveries, both of which were thought to be safe and infinitely useful. We now know that this one individual, the epitome of the specialist scientist, is possibly responsible for more environmental destruction than any one individual on the planet.

In all of these cases, specialists touted the advantages of certain products and chemicals, and the industrial and consumer audiences deemed the expertise of these professionals to be sufficient. Because no one had taken a holistic, precautionary look at the situation and studied the products' potential consequences on a broader scale, the results were devastating.

Such specialist thinking can be found in many sectors: economic theories of the leading economists that are now proving to be disastrous; industrial agriculture practices by leading "agriculture czars" that promoted a green revolution now being understood as lowering the overall long-term capacity of nations to feed themselves; medical and pharmaceutical experts creating "superbugs" through short-sighted use of antibacterial agents. It is easy to go on.

DEFINING THE POLYMATH

The American Heritage Dictionary defines the polymath as "a person of great and varied learning." The word stems from the Greek term "polumathes" and literally means "having learned much." The idea of the polymath returns to aspects of Renaissance Humanism and the notion that people should try to embrace all knowledge and develop themselves intellectually as fully as possible. Individuals like Alberti, Da Vinci, Copernicus and Goethe come to mind as icons of polymathy.

When I think of the polymath, I envision someone slightly different than a modern-day version of a Renaissance man or woman. True, a modern polymath is someone with at least a working knowledge of all primary specialties within a given field as well as basic knowledge of other fields. This individual is able to look holistically at a problem in order to make informed long-term decisions. She should be skeptical of solutions that seem to play out only in "lab tests" and that seem to defy common sense.

The modern polymath must part philosophical company with other aspects of Renaissance Humanism – namely, by rejecting the notion that mankind is at the center of the universe and the pinnacle of creation. It is this very hubris that led to many of the destructive habits of our species. The "Green Warrior" learns not to assume our species' superiority, but to understand how we fit into the larger creation of which we are a part – equal in importance and equally sacred with all life.

PURSUING TRUE INTEGRATION: THE POLYMATH APPROACH

Simply put – don't specialize – diversify

Although "integrated design" is a hot topic in the building industry, and many talented professionals claim to live by this model, true integration is actually quite rare in design professions or any professions for that matter. Indeed, while the trend toward integration is growing, the phrase itself – like "sustainability" before it – is often co-opted by otherwise well-meaning individuals who lack a genuine commitment or the required skill set to put integrated design or thinking into actual practice.

To use architecture again as an example for how "integrated thinking" fits into the bigger picture, let us look at various design approaches:

- **Traditional Design.** "Traditional" design as practiced by most architects and engineers can be described as a somewhat linear approach, in which various members of the team – architects, engineers and contractors all practice primarily alone in silos. The architect designs the building, the mechanical engineer specifies and sizes the "right" mechanical or structural systems, and the contractor prices the design and builds it. With, at times, very little overlap, it is no wonder that conflicts and problems can emerge. Environmental issues that cross disciplines are typically left unaddressed.

- **Semi-integrated Design – "conventional green building."** As green building has become more popular, it has become apparent that the old "silos" between various disciplines have needed to be broken down. And yet old habits die hard. Most green buildings, especially those projects using the LEED rating system, boast a certain amount of design integration. There tends to be relatively good collaboration and helpful relationships among specialists. This connection is what typically passes for true integrated design and yet it is a far cry from the kind of process needed to produce truly transformative projects. In these examples the team typically lacks a true polymath working as team leader. The disciplines while now "talking to each other" are still primarily sticking to their own silos and are not helping each other with decisions and designs.

- **Integrated Design.** Here we see a truly cyclical approach led by integrated thinkers who possess knowledge of, and insight into, the broader context. The polymath is involved in the early phases of development, and continues to lead the project until its completion. The architect plays a more signficant role in engineering and the engineer a more significant role in architecture. The contractor is an integral part of the team, helping with design ideas and working as part of the team on construction detailing. From beginning to end all disciplines work together.

To achieve true green design, the team must take an integrated approach guided by at least one integrated thinker who has been trained to think and work as a polymath. Now branch out to other disciplines, other fields. Again, it is most often the polymath who is missing in critical discussions. As you work on your transformation consider the idea that your role will not be to specialize, but to be a powerful generalist helping to bring the world of specialists together to more grounded, thoughtful and robust solutions.

THE JOURNEY TO POLYMATHY

Treat a man as he is and he will remain as he is. Treat a man as he can and should be and he will become as he can and should be.
—Goethe

The idea of becoming a polymath comes with the realization that it is a journey and not a destination as it is with specialization. As the saying goes, the more you know, the more you realize what you do not know – earning a degree is the destination of the specialist – a continuum of learning is the domain of the polymath.

Reading, writing, analyzing great works and studying the masters across a variety of fields are all excellent ways to begin to think like a polymath. Being open to a life of continual learning is key to the journey. One of the most beautiful things about pursuing a career in green building or sustainability is that it offers the potential for continual learning and fascinating linkages between disciplines and fields – provided you are open to it.

Since I began studying architecture, I have always been interested in the topic of daylight. The idea of using natural light to illuminate the interior of a space in a way that was more effective and energy-efficient is greatly appealing. I have seen how daylight, properly harnessed by a skilled craftsperson, can elevate architecture to the profound. One only has to look at some of the works by Finnish architectural master Alvar Aalto to understand this phenomenon. Aalto's modern designs are bright and wonderfully daylit. As a designer he understood light as an essential part of his design palette.

So throughout my career I have made it a task to learn everything I can about how to accomplish effective and beautiful daylighting design. After fifteen years of study, direct application and mentorship

Mount Angel Abbey Library by Alvar Aalto

with some of the country's top daylighting consultants, I am still learning and loving it. To someone new to the topic it might seem quite simple – simply add some windows to a room.

Windows bring in light – case closed.

On more thoughtful reflection, however, a lot of issues arise. Working from the inside-out, one might ask the following:

Are windows the best choice? Are there also skylights and suntubes to consider? If a window should be used, how big? Where on a wall should it be placed? What properties should the window have? How many windows are enough?

Windows bring in visible light but also ultraviolet light and heat. Of course, they let out heat and privacy too.

To control these factors there are many types of window properties – coatings and films, frit patterns, gas fills – literally hundreds of options to consider from dozens of manufacturers, each with strengths and weaknesses.[1] There are also an infinite number of architectural solutions that can be used to control light and heat gain or heat loss – overhangs, lightshelves, fins, screens, insulating shutters, louvers and more – each with its own issues ranging from construction details for long-term durability to how you will clean the windows once they are installed. To make it more interesting, daylight is not a static thing like a light bulb that is either on or off. It is infinitely variable – hour-by-hour, throughout the year – and changing throughout the year.

To understand daylight, one must then understand climate and weather – the effects of clouds or sunny days, winter and summer solstices and equinoxes – for each of five façades (east, west, south and north as well as the roof of the building). Each is different in terms of the sun's position, the amount of light available under different conditions – even the color of the light must be understood. Most likely, the same windows should not be used on all façades of a single structure for the simple reason that light conditions and sunlight are not the same on all sides of the building. How does all of this then change if your orientation is not exactly orthogonal – or if your building shape is not regular? How is it influenced by adjacent buildings – their shape, height and color?

Becoming a daylighting consultant also means digging up old physics textbooks, suddenly made more fascinating through practical

---

[1] After several years of studying glazing and its properties, I decided to write a manual about it and in 2004 published The Dumb Architect's Guide to Glazing Selection, a fun and informative primer on how to pick glazing. www.ecotonedesign.com

application, as one now has to really understand how light behaves, reflects, refracts and diffuses under different conditions and through different materials. Moving back from outside to inside it is important to understand the properties of dozens of typical building materials in terms of how they interact with light.

What color should your walls be and what surface texture? Will they cause glare? Will they increase or decrease light intensity and by how much?

The answers to so many of these questions then interact with a whole matrix of additional questions. What kind of space is the light coming into? What activities occur within it? How much light is needed and when? Who is using the space and for what end? – which involves understanding the schedules and equipment used by people inside the building. Will they use computers? Will they do work that requires even lighting or high levels or possibly low levels of light? How tall or wide is the room? What objects or structures might interfere or interact with the light inside the space? How does the daylight interact with the electric lighting within the space? A question that now brings us into the field of lighting design and electrical engineering!

What kind of lighting is used, since different light sources have different colors and properties to consider? Are there lighting controls available to dim the lights? Are there task lights or just ambient lights? Indirect or direct lighting? How many footcandles or lux[2] is required for safety, for code or expected by the client?

Interactions then occur with the mechanical engineer. How much heat gain or loss is the daylight responsible for? How does this interact with the size of mechanical systems? How does the lighting/daylighting loads affect how the building itself behaves and uses energy? How does

[2] Footcandles and lux are measurements of the amount of light in a space.

daylight contribute to the aesthetics of the space? To how people feel? To how productive they are? Can they control the light or is it fixed? Understanding the psychological dimensions of light suddenly takes on new meaning.

Our journey then takes us into the human eye itself and biology – how we see, how we see as we age, how to minimize glare or veiling reflections and on and on. Simple math tells us that there are trillions of possible combinations.

Is it as simple as putting a window in a room?

Yes and no.

The answer depends on the quality you are expecting. But taking daylighting to the level of art while minimizing energy use and environmental impact is a lifetime journey that takes one into multiple fields.

This is, of course, just one single example. My own map of discovery was not linear; it was extremely messy. Sometimes it was planned and sometimes it was simply found. But as I really began to understand daylighting not as a specialist but as a generalist, it became possible to see how this one discipline fit into a larger whole as I continued similar explorations related to material selection, energy efficiency, indoor air quality, water conservation and site design – all important aspects of green design. Who said you stop planning your education when you graduate from college?

THE ASCENDANCY

In architecture, those who can convey large amounts of information through a simple conceptual sketch are highly skilled at harnessing "the power of the parti." Architectural polymaths are able to sum up the essence of even the most multi-faceted structure in a simple and elegant diagram. If one has a deep enough grasp of a building's complexities and can explain the relationships between the parts of the design via a parti, (a sketch or a cartoon encapsulating the concept), then that person is acting as a polymath for that particular project. Conversely, if such an individual can not, in fact, create a parti despite his or her skill – then what is typically revealed is that the project is lacking some fundamental coherence that will result in it being less than successful.

Given the growing sense of environmental urgency and an increasing awareness of interconnected social, economic and environmental problems, the ascendancy of the polymath is more than a hopeful prediction – it is an inevitability. As one who understands how to marry our needs with those of our surroundings, the polymath will be in great demand. As such, it is incumbent upon all of us to educate, groom and value the generalist – both to recast education and our expectations of ourselves. We must work to change the way that our culture values specialists as something equal to but not better than a real generalist. Someone who understands multiple languages instead of just one language brings great value to any cultural understanding, as each language carries information that does not translate. The architect who does not understand engineering is as limited as the engineer who does not appreciate architecture and design.

As you prepare for your own zugunruhe, imagine a world where economists were also trained as biologists. Imagine a world where developers were also trained as artists and where MBAs were also trained as social workers. How then would our world be different? Knowing what you know about your own education – where should you turn next – not to necessarily dig deeper – but to broaden and understand the whole?

GWERSI III

In nature, diversity breeds resilience.

The same is true for our own resilience as people.

Therefore, seek first to become well-rounded in knowledge and training.

Less important are degrees and letters and the need to specialize.

Continually look for experiences outside of your current field of understanding, as the health of our inner dimensions – happiness, creativity and peace – are dependent upon being connected to an expanding network of experiences.

GWERSI IV

Chart your path to polymathy.

Learning should be a meandering path — book-to-book, experience-to-experience.

It should be charted generally but not absolutely, and it should jump field-to-field,

Discipline-to-discipline as new knowledge is needed.

The notion of "that's not my area" is outdated. It is always in our field if we care to learn.

STRUCTURAL CHANGES REQUIRED:
CHALLENGING OUR FUNDAMENTAL STRUCTURES

"Nobody has energy for outrage when you're trying to raise kids, hold down a job, pay your mortgage."

—ELIZABETH MAY, FORMER PRESIDENT, SIERRA CLUB CANADA

CROSSING YOUR SAHARA

Every year, thrush nightingales prepare for a journey that takes them from Sweden to South Africa. Along the way, they have to cross the great Sahara desert – and essentially survive without food and with little water for the five days it takes them to fly over the great desicated expanse. They survive by stopping and building up energy reserves at the edge of the Sahara, taking time at this crucial point in their journey to add more than 20 percent extra fat to their body mass, thereby making a significant change to their physical make-up by building in reserves.

When it is our turn to make a great journey, at the scale that I think is represented by the term Zugunruhe, signifying profound life changes, we often start out with lofty goals full of ambition. But often, after a period of time – usually within a few weeks – we find ourselves slipping back into old familiar patterns and the change we seek begins to elude us. When we reach that metaphorical moment when it is time to cross our own "Saharas" we find that we lack the inner reserves required. Despite clear goals and the best of plans, we find that deep-rooted changes are hard and significant inertia pulls us back into familiar ways of life. It is almost as if there is a system working against us.

Which is funny, because in many ways, there is.

THE DEEP GREEN PARADIGM SHIFT

Being green is unquestionably fashionable these days. And it is about time. But how many people deeply practice the green lifestyle that they preach or would like to live? Many people simply do not know what to change or how to prioritize the changes in their lives – and others, full of good intentions and a good conceptual understanding of environmental issues, continue to struggle to live an environmentally responsible life because they are working against the very systems or structures that support their lifestyles. Some of these systems are patterns of their own making to be sure and yet others are much more ingrained patterns of society's making. It is quite difficult to live with a small eco-footprint within the parameters of American or Canadian culture. All North Americans inherit a supporting system and infrastructure that is wasteful and inefficient – designed at a time when resources seemed limitless, and concern for the environment was minimal. Good intentions are not enough to be green when every basic decision seems to put you in a car or have you use energy created by coal or makes you a consumer of goods traveling halfway around the globe. It is not surprising that many committed environmentalists find themselves swimming upstream and having to make seemingly significant sacrifices to feel better about their life choices.

Falling short of best-laid plans is, of course, not unique to the green movement. We have all made New Year's resolutions we have failed to keep, pledged ourselves to fitness plans or diets we have not maintained and committed ourselves to chores we leave uncompleted. Most of these examples are small lessons in repeated failure (and not the valuable kind profiled in Chapter 7 of this book). We fail at these efforts because they usually require that we make difficult structural changes within our lives that we are not prepared to acknowledge or we are not even aware of. Without challenging underlying structures our "change efforts" remain superficial and it is only a matter of time before the inevitable takes over. And yet we keep trying and failing to make change at this superficial level because the deeper core changes either elude us or seem too difficult. Most of us live the lifestyles we do because, at a fundamental level, it is working for us. These lifestyles may be unhealthy and they might carry a significant environmental burden but at some important level they are easier to continue with than to change. We then keep resolving to make changes within our current life paradigm by pledging to simply be "better" or "more disciplined".

This reality gets to the heart of why it is so hard to be truly green. Being thoroughly green requires more than a simple belief in the value of environmental responsibility. A majority of North Americans "value" environmental issues when asked in opinion polls –but few change their lifestyles or work because of it. True stewardship requires more than simply "trying harder" while continuing to live the lives we currently do. It means asking ourselves extremely hard questions about what structural changes we need to make and challenging major societal systems that, by design, make it easier to pollute and consume than it does to conserve and preserve. It feels Sisyphean, and many of us give up when the mountain gets too steep and the rock continues to roll backward.

But does it have to be this way? Or is it possible to make structural changes to our lives whereby our happiness and well-being improves while dramatically lowering our own impacts effortlessly? Getting ready to cross our Sahara requires examining our underlying structures so that we do not burn the reserves we have within the first few miles of the journey.

In the late 1990s, I sought to write a book on the subject of personal sustainability – in some ways an earlier version of this book. I wanted to partner with a good friend of mine, a leader in the field of Life Cycle Assessment (LCA) with whom I was working extensively on a project in Montana called the EpiCenter. We spent a great deal of time discussing how we could explore the ways in which individuals can put in balance all aspects of their lives – environmental, social, economic and physical – to conduct truly sustainable, healthy, resource-efficient lives. It sounded great, and we were both genuinely interested in the topic, but despite our efforts, we just could not pull off the project.

Why? For several reasons I believe. First, both of our busy schedules made it difficult to find time to collaborate on the book, so it was constantly being pushed back – we kept resolving to try harder. Secondly, as we continued to discuss it, we kept bumping into the harsh reality that up until that point we personally had not done a very good job in our own lives of demonstrating the very things we wanted to write about in the book!

There is an old joke that says that messed up people are those that end up being therapists because they truly do understand dysfunction. Perhaps this was true for my friend and I relative to leading a sustainable life – except it just did not work for us. Our lifestyles at that time did not deeply enough exemplify the message of sustainability and balance we wanted to present in the book and, as a result, the content would have lacked integrity.

The harder I tried to work on it, the more that "life" got in the way. It was not that I was slacking off; quite the opposite, in fact. I was extremely busy doing good work, and devoting my efforts to the industry of sustainability. But I lacked the discipline to achieve true sustainability in the way I balanced my life and its demands. I recognized the goal; I just could not reach it for reasons I had not yet grasped.

When it comes to making lifestyle changes in a quest to be green, it is not enough to recycle or use reusable shopping bags. We must, in fact, change long-time patterns we have adopted based on where we live, what we eat, what we do for a living and how we spend our leisure time. The reality is that in a consumer-dominated culture, it is far easier to consume than it is to be frugal. It is much easier to be a global consumer than a committed locovore. Pledging to make better use of public transportation in most American cities, for example, is a big commitment but often turns into an even bigger hassle in communities with excessive sprawl and infrastructure that is not interconnected.

Without a highly connected and well-designed public infrastructure most people who can afford it simply fall back into the ease and reliability of driving.

THE JAGUAR AND THE SPARROW – A HUMOROUS LESSON

When I was a young boy, I spent endless hours playing with small toy cars, zooming them around imaginary racetracks and dirt roads throughout the living room. While I had an impressive array of various makes and models, I always gravitated toward the sport cars, whose sleek lines and gentle curves fascinated me. As I got a bit older, I gradually lost my interest in toy cars, and I never developed much of a fascination for engines or for tinkering under hoods of any kind. However, I continued to be attracted to the aesthetics of certain "real" cars and my head would turn when beautiful models would drive by. Perhaps it was the "British" connection to my commonwealth roots, but one make in particular captured my heart: the Jaguar XJ6. This spectacular specimen seemed the most elegant and stately of all cars on the road in my adolescent mind. A show I used to watch back in the early 1980s called The Equalizer had the protagonist driving this very car and I believed it to be the epitome of cool.

Unfortunately, when I reached driving age, the only wheels available to me were on my father's old chevy station wagon – about as far away from automotive elegance as possible. One day when I was seventeen, I promised myself that I would someday sit in my own Jaguar.

Fast forward a few years.

For most of my college experience, my only mode of transportation was a wonderful Cannondale mountain bike. I did everything on that bike: rode to school, traveled to friends' houses, even grocery shopped using a very large backpack that I filled to capacity. I lived in Eugene, Oregon

– one of the few towns in America where bicycles are seen as a welcome mode of transportation rather than a nuisance to the automobile. Almost all of the streets in Eugene had dedicated bicycle lanes, which made biking easy and safe. The city also had a wonderful network of trails and paths that extended across the city separate from automobile traffic. The weather also helped, being warm enough for bike travel almost all year. Even the notoriously rainy winters were bearable if one had a good set of rain clothes. Biking was a transportation solution that offered exercise, cost virtually nothing and minimized excess, as it was impossible to carry anything of consequence on a bike. Impulse buys were not an option. The resulting benefits were clear: I was in great shape and living a fairly benign existence. When it was time for my weekly grocery shop I would load up my giant backpack – putting milk and other heavy items at the bottom – it was funny at times, given all the weight I could often barely get on my bike for my ride home.

During college, I also lived for a time in Scotland, where even a bike was unnecessary since everything I needed was within walking distance of my home. European cities have historically been designed for people rather than for cars and as a result I thoroughly enjoyed walking everywhere. Living in communities where the best way to travel was on foot or by bike, I very easily forgot about my personal promise to own a certain British car.

But in the mid-1990s, I moved to Kansas City, Missouri, a decision that was to have significant structural ecological implications for me. For six months, still very much in the mode of bike and pedestrian living, I attempted to live without a car in Kansas City. I took the bus to and from work and borrowed rides to events and meetings whenever I needed to get around. The problem was that Kansas City is heavily suburbanized and is plagued with the second highest vehicle miles traveled in America behind Houston. Despite good efforts the Kansas City bus network leaves much to be desired.

As my job became more demanding, it became incredibly difficult and time-consuming to be car-less. Getting to work was challenging enough; getting to meetings was nearly impossible, given Kansas City's sprawling auto-centric infrastructure and poor public transportation system. I concluded that I had to get myself a car just to participate in a Midwestern life and work.

Suddenly, a whole new set of possibilities opened up. What kind of car should I buy? At the time I was not committed enough to owning a new car so I began to look for used ones. I looked at a lot of cars but I was not very excited. But after two weeks of looking fate tempted me.

I learned that a neighbor was selling his beautiful four-door 1986 Jaguar XJ6...the dream car from my youth. He was willing to part with it for less than $5000 (my max budget) and, after talking with him and looking at it...and then test driving it...against my better judgment, the little boy in me gave in on impulse. I bought it with cash (okay, a check) on the spot.

Between the moment I first held the keys in my hand and the moment twenty-four months later when the car literally burst into flames while I was driving it and had to be extinguished by a fire truck before it could explode (which is, in and of itself, another story but offers wonderful metaphorical significance to this one), I was conflicted and unsettled about my decision.

I will not deny how much fun it was to drive the Jaguar. It handled better than anything I had ever driven, and simply floated on the highway. Parked in the sun, its double headlights gleamed back at me. But I was never able to enjoy it fully, given my ever-present guilt that I had made an irresponsible choice. How could I – an environmentalism teacher and activist – justify such a possession? Worse still, I was actually ashamed at how much I felt a part of me needed the car. I needed its beauty, which complemented its utility. If you are going to own a car surely you should have something that is fun to drive, beautiful to look at and comfortable? I have always believed that we crave form in function, as so few of the items that surround us have been built with loving design. The Japanese have a saying that I have always appreciated: "Nothing is beautiful that does not have function, and nothing is functional that does not have beauty."

I fulfilled my promise to myself that I made when I was seventeen — but, of course, life is not as simple as it was back then. My love-hate relationship with the Jaguar continued for two solid years. I found myself justifying its place in my life by driving it as little as possible. What a conflicted decision! Buying something and then trying not to use it! Putting fewer than 3000 miles annually on such a gas-guzzler meant that I was responsible for significantly fewer emissions – 5000 pounds of carbon dioxide every year, based on my calculations – than the average American. Still, I felt hypocritical.

So when the car spontaneously caught on fire (yes, it is true —picture five foot flames coming from the hood), I took it as a signal from the universe to radically change my decision. A car in Kansas City was still a necessity, but I now sought a solution that was as green as humanly possible – yet one that would still be fun to drive and beautiful to look at. Turned out this was hard to find. Prior to the availability of hybrids there were not many options in an automotive landscape that had not seen improved fuel efficiency in a couple of decades. I decided to go electric and I soon found myself focused on a new company in California producing quirky little electric vehicles called the Corbin Sparrow.

The Sparrow was a single-seat electric vehicle that offered style, and cost-efficiency, all wrapped up in a nice green package. It zipped around the city with ease, providing me with all the space my briefcase and I ever needed. In terms of pollution impact, it got the equivalent of 180 miles to the gallon even with Kansas City's dirty electricity fuel mix. Once I made the switch from the beastly Jaguar to the gentle Sparrow, I could not be happier – my internal conflict was over.

I was proud of my new form of transportation, and of my own structural shift. Shaking the Jaguar monkey off my back was easier than I expected it to be. The Sparrow made me proud, and proved that small changes can actually have huge impacts – and it was not a compromise – it was an improvement. Its lessons did not end there however, for learning to drive an electric car teaches you how to drive differently. Since range was limited, I soon began adjusting how I drove to maximize mileage and found that I could increase its performance considerably. With the Jaguar, I powered up hills, but I now learned to coast, draft and avoid stopping – a technique now popularly known as "hyper-miling." Many people find that with the right techniques that they can get 80 mpg out of cars designed to get 35. It was fun and more intellectually stimulating than any driving I had ever done. The Sparrow changed my habits and connected me with the consequences of my actions more directly.

In hindsight, of course, my decision to get rid of the Jaguar was a no-brainer. Owning and driving it ran counter to everything I taught and believed in about personal ecological responsibility. Abandoning the Jaguar and embracing the Sparrow required less of an adjustment on my part, for greater happiness and significantly lower environmental impact. Making a deep green decision did not then, nor does not now, have to mean giving up quality and beauty.

CLOSE TO HOME

How, then, do we go about changing the underlying structures of our lives, our cities and our culture in order to achieve personal sustainability? In my experience, it requires a combination of big

Corbin Sparrow

decisions. When I left my job as a principal at BNIM and moved west
to join Cascadia, I did so primarily because I wanted to increase the
rate at which I could affect real change in the building industry as
a whole rather than in individual projects. Going from a building-
by-building approach to a firm-by-firm approach in order to
spread the green gospel, I knew I could make a substantially bigger
difference. Doing so, however, required my family and me to make
some fundamental structural changes. When it was time to do so, I
reevaluated a host of issues that I wanted to change:

- We relocated from a car-centric community to a community
  where being a single-car household and relying on bicycles
  and mass-transit for some of our transportation needs were
  once again realistic and pleasant propositions.

- I structured my work schedule so that I could telecommute from home at least two or three days per week, dramatically cutting my gas consumption and maximizing the time I get to spend with my children – a critical goal that I felt I was not previously able to achieve.

- We found an existing house, built in the 1970s entirely from salvaged wood from a deconstructed warehouse, thereby considerably lowering the embodied energy of our structure. The house was also disconnected from the municipal water and sewer grid and operated sustainably within the water-balance of the site. The location of the home meant that I almost never had to drive on the freeway; I was able to use ferry and foot power to get to work in Seattle when needed.

- We created an environment in which our children would have considerable access to nature – deer, fish, forest and water – essential, I believe, to raising children who will steward the earth's resources.[1]

I was fortunate enough for all the stars to align in order for me to make these alterations in my personal structure. I am closer now to meeting my own sustainability goals while staying on track with my professional aspirations. Make no mistake, I acknowledge that this is easier said than done for the majority of people. But that is precisely the point here. For me, it took examining my lifestyle and reconciling the reality of the structures in place that were making it challenging to meet my goals. This process is not only possible for personal change but for organizational change as well.

In architecture, for example, when a firm greens its standard specifications and details, it ensures a structural change in the

---

[1] Check out a book on the reading list entitled *Nature Deficit Disorder*.

way its work affects the surrounding community for every single building it does. Codifying the right changes rather than inefficient changes has considerable power. Similarly, municipalities or states that require LEED Certification for municipal projects codify a set of values that end up giving the taxpayer considerably more value – better buildings with lower energy and operating costs that save millions over their life. These are all strong arguments for regulation, as mandated changes cause early-stage scrambling but result in long-term innovation and improvement. Every time industry screams that higher standards will "bankrupt" them, the opposite has proved true. Asian automakers are now reaping the benefits or our inability to make structural changes to our U.S. – and Canadian – made vehicles by successfully lobbying against higher Café standards. We adapt to change when it is forced upon us and, in the case of lowering our environmental footprint, we are usually better off for it since it often makes us re-examine basic assumptions and improve our current paradigm. If the green path seems like the more difficult one on which to tread, that is because it is operating within a paradigm never intended to be light on the land. But under a new paradigm, designed from the ground up to be environmentally responsible while also meeting other requirements, then, in fact, it can be quite easy to do the right thing.

FIGHTING TO CHANGE THE SYSTEM(S)

The environmental problems of today are most often caused by systems, infrastructure, technologies and designs where environmental impact was never a prime consideration or was not deemed important enough to influence the outcome. Environmental impacts – both positive and negative – are usually unintended consequences of the structures, industries and lifestyles we create, not a conspiracy to pollute our air or water. People often do not know better, or fail to see the connections, or have found a way to rationalize that the impact they are creating is for some larger good.

The good news is that it does not take a nation of environmental radicals to create a truly sustainable society. We do not have to convert everyone or even make everyone environmentally aware in order to succeed. Rather, it requires us to make significant changes in the underlying systems of society, so that as people go about their lives they are doing things that naturally have positive rather than negative impact. Why should everyone be constantly thinking of environmental impact when they are just trying to feed themselves or get to work? Why can we not simply get to a place where environmentally benign or beneficial decisions are par for the course? Where doing the right thing is the easier thing? This is the destination we need to hold in our minds. To get there, some major structural changes are required and this change, I believe, has to be a fundamental part of the work of our collective Zugunruhe. First, make your own internal structural changes as effectively as you can and then prepare for the larger work ahead of all of us – changing the very systems that define modern societies. It is time to prepare.

G W E R S I   V

Look deeply for habits, patterns and systems that support all aspects of your life – where you live, what you do, how you travel and what you eat – and explore the possibility of a complete change, not an incremental one.

Strive for each action to reinforce the kind of impact you wish to have.

Find holistic solutions that simultaneously solve multiple things you want to address.

It is your life.

You are not trapped in your reality.

GWERSI VI

In your business or work,

Find opportunities to codify environmental improvements.

Reexamine standard procedures, rules of thumb and corporate policies.

Institutionalized restoration can work as easily as institutionalized degradation.

Challenge and question.

Redefine.

05

NESTED TIME ON THE BRAIN'S RIGHT SIDE:
HOLISTIC THINKING, TIME MANAGEMENT AND MAKING RISOTTO

It is human nature for us to tackle challenges by first attempting to define the problem at hand within the context of our previous experiences and existing knowledge. We can not help it; that is all we know, so that is all the information we have with which to deal with new situations. The obvious problem with this approach, however, is that it limits us to a set of possible answers that may not be suitable for the questions we need to ask. We end up working within a construct that defines us – and imprisons us.

When we seek to make real change in our lives and in our businesses, we must begin by thinking beyond the limits of our own experiences, and by turning our own conventional thinking on its head. But how do we do this?

DRAWING ON THE RIGHT SIDE

In 1979, an art teacher named Betty Edwards published a groundbreaking book called *Drawing on the Right Side of the Brain* after conducting research on the ways in which both hemispheres of the brain contribute to, as well as hinder, learning. In the book, she demonstrates the powerful truth that the left side of our brain, which is devoted to logical and analytical thinking, actually hinders our ability to learn to draw and visualize precisely because it "thinks" it knows how to solve the problem of drawing when in fact it does not. Most people experience frustration upon attempting to draw and very few pursue it further than what elementary school requires. When one says," I can't draw," it is actually the left brain that can not draw. Edwards' techniques have shown thousands of people how to "shut off" their left brains and learn with their right brains, allowing even those with no apparent artistic talent to make dramatic leaps in creative performance in short periods of time. Techniques include drawing upside-down and obscuring elements of a picture so that the left brain does not try to "finish" an effort based on what it "knows." Edwards shows what is possible when we take ourselves out of the paradigm to which we have become accustomed – only then are we able to recognize the changes that need to take place. This observation is not to say that right brain dominant people get it and left brain people do not – not at all. We have all seen incredibly creative people unable to function and solve simple problems because they have not known when to change the way they think. We have two sides of our brain for a reason. It is time that we use both of them.

THE TIME OF YOUR LIFE – AN EXAMPLE

Time is a human-made construct that governs and restricts us. It has the power to become our greatest limiter, our biggest source of personal frustration and the greatest barrier between us and our ability to create profound change. From the time we are little, we are taught to think of time in a purely linear fashion. Like so many things in our lives, one thing happens after another, end of story, and we do not challenge it. When we look at time management from a new angle however, we give ourselves the power to drive major change in our own lives.

It is cliché to say that time is precious. Anything finite and limited is such. Add the increasing pace with which we insist on living and the countless tools that help us squeeze more into our days and it is no wonder everybody feels pinched. Time is a valuable commodity, yet how many of us really look at how we spend it? Do we do all we can to get the most out of the time we have? Is there a connection between the way we spend time and the quality of our lives and our happiness? And here is a big one: is there a significant environmental impact when we mismanage or lose track of our time? Let us take a look at a couple of reasons why we are so short on time.

REASON ONE – TEMPORAL PARASITICS

Most of us do not really understand where our time goes during any given day. To paraphrase my good friend Ron Perkins,[1] "You do not know what you do not measure, and what you do not measure you do not really understand." A big problem for most Americans is a phenomenon that I call temporal parasitics.

Parasitics is an energy efficiency term used to describe equipment that draws power even when not in use. Nearly every household appliance is a parasitic load once plugged in. A conventional television set, for example, draws electricity when plugged in, even while off, which costs its owners money and creates pollution. The primary justification for this particular parasitic is to keep the set's internal tube warm so that the picture appears as soon as the TV is turned on rather than taking several seconds to heat up. This momentary convenience – this brief time-saving advantage – drains energy all day and all night, year-round. Is instant gratification worth the pollution that is generated and money that is wasted to achieve it? The notion of holistic time management asks the same question.

In life, there are a million little things that we do each and every day in order to maintain our lifestyles. Our small decisions support our big ones regarding where we live, what we do to support ourselves and how we define success. We ignore these seemingly insignificant decisions because we consider them trivial; we think of them as unnecessary and we do not take them into account when we make important choices. But I believe we should make them visible because, in sum, they account for the vast majority of our wasted time. They suck away time; they are temporal parasitics.

---

[1] Ron Perkins is the CEO of a consulting firm called SuperSymmetry USA and is one of the most innovative engineers on the continent.

Any major life decision comes complete with a whole package of hidden temporal parasitics that are either small or large, depending on the course of action. Whatever their magnitude, they have serious implications. One need only look at the number of Americans whose financial liabilities hurl them into endless cycles of work and debt reduction to see how temporal parasitics have the capacity to ruin health, happiness and home life. For when you are in debt, you are not in complete control of your time.

For many Americans, the decision to buy into the "American dream" has been disastrous – for their families as well as the environment – as it is often driven more by a desire for possessions and status than by genuine need. The typical dream scenario involves buying a large house in the suburbs, at least twice as big as the house the buyers grew up in (and now serving a smaller family) instead of living closer to work in a more integrated, multi-use neighborhood. This decision has led the average American to spend a significant amount of time and money each day commuting to work (and generating more emissions) and running errands made necessary by the great distances between services. Even more time is spent maintaining the oversized homes and hiring help to clean it, which of course requires more work hours to fund.

Other examples roll in:

- We accept jobs that require overtime or indirect work-related time in order to generate more income to pay for the mortgages on the big houses.

- We purchase additional vehicles to shuttle us to and from our jobs, often spending additional time looking for parking or being stuck in rush-hour traffic.

- We invest in elaborate wardrobes to support our professional positions and because of a lack of time spend more time and money on dry cleaning and laundering.

- We spend more time eating out since we do not have time to cook at home.

And the time-eating cancer grows....

Like their energy counterparts, temporal parasitics usually impose an environmental burden as well. For each mile it crawls through traffic, the average automobile produces between .5 to 1.5 pounds of carbon dioxide, which also contributes to the creation of ground level ozone, particulates and other threats to our health. Eating "convenience" food – including pre-packaged meals and menu items from fast food restaurants – is as bad for our health as it is for the environment, given the energy and resources used to package, process and ship the food as well as the industrialized agricultural systems needed to support it.

REASON TWO – TEMPORAL DILUTION

Temporal dilution refers to activities that we do not need to do, and many times do not even particularly want to do, yet we do out of habit, boredom or stress. They do not add value to our lives, but we seek them out nonetheless. For many people, watching television is a great example. Certainly there can be quite valuable programming, but too many Americans and Canadians use television like junk-food, endlessly flipping channels and not digesting anything meaningful or intellectually nutritious. I call it temporal dilution because it typically refers to activities that we do not notice or account for but, bit-by-bit, siphon time away from more meaningful things. Many of our unproductive or unfulfilling activities occur just a little bit at a time, and therefore we do not experience their cumulative effects consciously. We are not aware in the moment how much time we spend – or waste, depending on your perspective – engaging in these activities. We do know, however, that we always feel the time crunch and there never seems to be enough hours in the day to do all that we want and need to do. Time dilution makes it difficult for us to see the incentive to change. We justify enormous hours away: "What does it matter if I watch an hour of television every day or commute for forty-five minutes to my job? That is not much time, and many people watch much more television than I do and have much longer commutes." But here is the rub: rationalizations such as these prevent us from devoting our time and living our lives the way we would like to – and being effective in the coming years ahead will require us to be much more consciously in control of our time.

With time dilution, we do not notice things even though their cumulative effects are just as damaging to our health and well-being as if they happened all at once.

Let us begin to think on "the right side of our brain" and take a closer look at how we spend our time.

What if we had to lump together all the time we spend in, say, a year on each time-diluting activity, and examine how our twelve month schedule would map out? I believe that such an exercise would make us all learn a few things about the priorities that we set and how to get on the path to becoming green warriors.

The typical American working adult has the following habits:[2]

- Sleeps an average of 7.5 hours each day
- Works 8 hours per day

---

[2] These statistics are averages based on a variety of sources. Readers are encouraged to insert their own hours to get a sense of how it may work for them.

- Spends 1.2 hours commuting to and from work
- Spends 1.1 hours daily eating and drinking (although increasingly while commuting to and from work)
- Devotes 2.6 hours to leisure and sports every day
- Spends 1 hour a day in the bathroom (doing all sorts of things)
- Watches 3.5 hours of TV each day
- Cares for others for 1.2 hours each day
- Engages in other household activities for 1 hour each day
- Spends the remaining time in miscellaneous activities[3]

Now let us look at this another way. Let us say that each year you had to perform each of these tasks in succession instead of in little daily or weekly increments that you do not think about, stopping only to sleep for your requisite 7.5 hours, but spending every other waking moment performing each particular task. What would it look like over the course of the year?

- From January 1st-24th you would spend all of your time simply driving to and from work – by yourself (since most North Americans drive by themselves in their car) and during three of those days you would spend all your waking hours completely stuck in traffic!

---

[3] In case you are wondering why this does not add up to 24 hours, keep in mind that these are all averages from various sources and not from a real person. Each person's mix, based on current understanding of time and physics, would add up to 24 hours. There may also be some "double-counting" as people do tend to do multiple activities at once, such as eating while watching TV.

- From January 25th to May 20th you would work 16-hour days in a job that you probably do not like.[4]

- From May 21st – July 31st you would watch TV continuously – much of it alone and most of it barely entertaining – and a good two solid weeks will be just commercials!

- August 1st – August 20th you will spend in the bathroom, doing whatever it is you do in there!

- August 21st – September 10th you will spend time doing chores including shopping, cleaning, doctor visits and other errands, none of which you wanted to do in the first place!

Now wait right there. It is now September 10th. Summer's over and fall has arrived and you still have not spent any quality time with your kids, your spouse or for yourself. And sadly, when you do carve out those times, you end up with less than a month for each. What is wrong with that picture?

How do you spend your time? If these were your patterns, would you make profound changes on your own behalf or for your kids? If you learned that you spent a significant portion of your time in ways that also used considerable energy and increased your ecological footprint, would you find it easier to change? When you look at your time-use patterns, ask yourself how your job choice affects your time. How does where you live affect the hours you spend doing things you do not want to do (such as commute)? Are there activities you would like to be able to spend more time doing? The key is to be aware of things that take time and have a time-oriented ripple effect, drawing on our physical and emotional reserves and making us less effective in other areas.

---

[4] Most polls in the US show less than 40 percent job satisfaction numbers.

The sad reality is that we do not notice life passing us by when it does so in little increments. As a result, we tend to make less time for the really important things because we are busy frittering away time on the mundane – what Antoine De Saint-Exupéry calls "matters of consequence."

One is reminded of the life lesson summarized and passed around in recent years via email, in which a professor stands before his classroom with a large vessel, a pile of rocks, a bag of sand and a pitcher of water. He fills the vessel to capacity with rocks, then asks the students if it is full. "Yes," they reply. "No more rocks will fit." He then adds sand, which fills the spaces between the rocks. "Is it full now?" he asks. "Yes, now it is full," the students say. Finally, he adds water, which spreads easily throughout the sand. "Now this vessel is full," he announces. "The moral here is clear: we must start by taking care of the big things in life – family, friends, our health, our well-being – because there will always be room for the little things, as they can take up the remaining spaces."

WHAT TO DO?

The sustainability crisis today is a lifestyle crisis, as the ecological problems we face are caused largely by the little decisions millions of us make each day. Yes, consumerism has played a large part, but perhaps just as insidious are our societal patterns that rob us of time while simultaneously causing great environmental impact. We are pulled away from our family lives, civic organizations, community involvement and activities that keep us grounded.

When we have opportunities or are forced to make lifestyle changes – what we do, where we live, how we get from one place to another – and consider the effects our choices have on the environment and our well-being, the connection between time parasitics and sustainability becomes clear. Most activities that eat away at our time also create an environmental burden. For example, the average suburban resident living in a detached home and commuting by car has an ecological footprint almost three times that of his urban counterpart who lives in an apartment and either walks or takes public transportation to work.

Obviously, it is not possible for each environmentally-aware individual to make radical changes all at once. The good news is that we can accomplish many of the same goals by using the nested problem solving approach.

NESTED PROBLEM SOLVING

Every once in a while, we make decisions that seem particularly sound – decisions made in a moment of grace that help solve multiple problems at once. I like to call this type of solution nested problem solving, as individual answers nest within others.

With practice, nested problem solving can become an everyday methodology in and of itself and it has the potential to greatly increase the quality of life we all seek. Once we become aware of the interconnectedness of our daily habits, our ability to manage time and the ecological impact of our decisions, nested solutions come more easily. Please note that this is not the same thing as "multi-tasking," which is merely doing different things at the same time usually none of it as well as you could do if you focused! Nested problem solving focuses on pairing or merging activities that are synergistic and enhance the result or the enjoyment in doing them. Truly nested solutions tend to be simultaneously good for our health, our pocketbooks and the environment. These solutions are a complete reversal from many habits that cost us a lot, have great environmental burdens and contribute to poor health and leave us with nested problems to be solved!

Nested solutions may be cultivated using such simple tools as daily to-do lists. I, for one, am a relentless list maker. I like to take a few moments in the evening to jot down the key tasks I know I need to accomplish the following day so that, wherever possible, I can group the items on my list into logical categories. This option helps cut down on wasted time, and helps me stay on track.[5] This type of system does not work for everyone, but anyone who wants to streamline time management can find his or her most effective method of nesting solutions[6].

They can also be cultivated by taking the time to reflect on all possible consequences that may occur from the action or task in question and asking "Is there a better way to approach this task that is healthier, more ecologically sound and inexpensive?" It requires a willingness to measure and understand the impacts of the current paradigm before simply changing it.

Naturally, the hardest part of the process is coming up with the solution, but most people are creative enough to come up with several appropriate solutions as soon as they broaden the context.

Unfortunately, many people are stuck in an all too common pattern, a spiraling of interconnected problems that leads to negative feedback loops. For example, the busy career person with no time to cook rarely eats at home – ironically spending almost the same time traveling to and from places to eat, often choosing unhealthy and environmentally disastrous fast food or packaged foods all the while spending at least twice the amount of money for nutritionally diminished fare. The person stuck in this pattern ends up needing to work more to pay for the habit of eating out and the stressful, wasteful cycle continues.

---

[5] Something for the right-brain thinker to work on and learn from the left-brain!

[6] For more on the power of list making see the book by Atul Guwande called the *Checklist Manifesto*.

We need to look for synergistic activities or synergistic ways of accomplishing our goals. The Buddhist Thich Nhat Hahn talks about using the mundane to practice the profound, not by multi-tasking but actually by focusing on the task at hand. As he says, "When you are doing the dishes, you should be doing the dishes!" Mindfulness produces its own nested solutions.

MAKING RISOTTO

To my mind, the idea that doing the dishes is unpleasant can occur only when you are not doing them. Once you are standing in front of the sink with your sleeves rolled up and your hands in warm water, it really is not so bad. I enjoy taking my time with each dish, being fully aware of the dish, the water, and each movement of my hands. I know that if I hurry in order to go and have a cup of tea, the time will be unpleasant and not worth living. That would be a pity, for each minute, each second of life is a miracle.
—Thich Nhat Hanh

Whenever I can, I take the time to cook an incredibly elaborate meal at home. I especially enjoy the act of chopping and preparing the ingredients, relishing the fresh raw scent of vegetables, onions and garlic on my hands. Although we have a garlic press, I do not use it in the preparation of one of these feasts, as I prefer to work by hand with an extra sharp knife cutting and slicing and setting each ingredient aside until I have a beautiful tray ready for cooking. For me, these culinary projects are all about delving fully and completely into the task of preparing food for my family and enjoying the process of turning raw ingredients into melded and enriched tastes through cooking. I simply lose myself in it, and it makes for a powerful metaphor in the idea of nested problem solving. While cooking "slow food," I am:

- Pursuing a treasured leisure activity

- Allowing myself time for reflection and stress relief

- Sharing this work (and the fruits of the labor) with loved ones

- Contributing to my health by using quality organic ingredients

- Reducing my environmental footprint, since hand-prepared, seasonal and locally sourced meals have less of an environmental impact than "quick and simple" packaged dishes with ingredients from all corners of the planet

Risotto

One of my best friends, who has seen me in my soiled apron and who shares similar appreciations for cooking, describes the process of taking the time to do things right as "making risotto." I now use the phrase as a metaphor for describing the action of losing yourself in any function that promotes quality of life and serves as a nested solution for health, environmental benefit and human interaction. For me, "making risotto" can be as simple as taking a long walk with my dog. Sometimes it is sitting down with a cup of tea and reading a good book for an hour instead of watching television. Making risotto is a directive to slow down, allow time to think and become proactive rather than reactive to our daily routines. Amazing things happen when we turn down our energy levels and do things more slowly and deliberately.

Needless to say, making risotto is a metaphor for green living. In the proverbial rat race, there is little time for anything but consumption and so-called progress. We are reactive rather than proactive, which means we rarely have the time to craft elegant and intelligent solutions.

And yet in the coming years, to address the challenges we will surely face, it is imperative that we have the time to create such compelling solutions. Mastering the "nested time on the brain's right side" becomes essential.

G W E R S I   V I I

Turn thinking on its head.

When stuck in a problem, change the paradigm by turning it upside down.

Think consciously of how your opposite would react and cultivate both your left and right brain modes of problem solving.

Stretch out of your comfort zone so that you are ready to change dramatically when it is most important.

GWERSI VIII

Be brave and look for the ideal solution in every endeavor.

It is not too much to ask for solutions to life's challenges that are healthy, environmentally sound and economically wise.

Slow down, aim for simplicity and make each decision count.

Practice mindfulness.

GWERSI IX

Take time to "make risotto" in all aspects of life.

Add flair and beauty to the tasks you face and revel in your ability to put your personal stamp on your creations.

Have fun with the little jobs you do, which make you better able to appreciate the more significant accomplishments that come along.

Enjoy the present, for that is all we have.

BEGINNING THE MIGRATION:
REFLECTION THEN SELF-PROJECTION

"If I accept you as you are, I will make you worse; however, if I treat you as though you are what you are capable of becoming, I help you become that."

—GOETHE

"No-one can make you feel inferior without your consent."

—ELEANOR ROOSEVELT

Before the start of any journey, a certain amount of preparation needs to be done. The more arduous and lengthy the journey, the more time spent packing and planning. Are essential supplies ready? Are routes planned? Is our gear in order? Perhaps most importantly, are we ready mentally for the challenge ahead?

When it comes to the journey of the green warrior — our ecological zugunruhe — preparing for the change at hand means that we need to be at our best, ready and prepared and in the proper frame of mind. We need to strike out with confidence in what we are capable of doing and with a clear and realistic mind of what we are ready to take on. Yet, too often people limit their own potential to create change in the future by being too self-critical and hard on themselves. They undersell what they are capable of and start the journey already with severe handicaps. They see everything they do as being inadequate and feel ashamed of their shortcomings – always striving and failing for some imagined ideal or unrealistic personal expectations. Some, even late in life, continue to hear the disapproving voices of their long-gone parents, teachers or coaches and carry a burden of unhealthy expectations and failures on their shoulders.

I have also met many others who mistakenly believe that they cannot make a difference in this world for the very reason that they do not feel like they measure up. Worse yet, they believe that they are incapable of changing themselves, and of moving beyond their own self-imposed limitations. By saying, "this is just the way I'm wired," "I do not have this expertise" or "I have nothing unique to add" or other concessions, they stifle their own ability to progress, grow and enable change in the world. If one looks inward and sees only weakness, that person's outward impacts will correlate. Such self-fulfilling prophecies are immoveable and tragic.

We also put too much stock in what others think of us and ratchet up or down (usually down) our own expectations and goals depending on what others we care about think we can accomplish. Usually what people think we can do are tempered by that individual's own baggage as others project their own limitations on what they think someone can achieve. And too often people judge our current abilities based on old history, not readily accepting the idea that people grow, change and mature. This is why "experts" often come from somewhere far away and why people feel like they need to leave their hometown to succeed. People can not get past the child they remember growing up with and they expect an expert to come fully formed.

While it might sound cliché, I believe that everyone can, in fact, make a significant difference to the current state of the world. Let me be clear: I do not mean to re-package the American mythology that suggests that anyone can do anything as long as the work ethic and the drive are there. On the contrary, I find that idea to be self-defeating and insulting. Not everyone can be president despite how hard they work. Not everyone can run a four-minute mile or become a millionaire. People have different abilities, backgrounds and opportunities available. And there is also luck or fate or both to consider. Yet all of us can become much greater than that which we are today, and contribute in significant ways based on the talents we do have and the opportunities that exist all around us. But it is our outlook and perception of ourselves that allow us to see how to apply the potential we have. The magic is in understanding how to harness a beautiful future through the proper understanding of our own potential, realistically and healthily assessed.

A SELF-AWARENESS PRIMER

"Knowing others is wisdom; knowing the self is enlightenment."
—Tao Te Ching

Old habits are difficult to break, which is why it is so hard to initiate fundamental changes in the way we perceive ourselves and our own potential. Following a few basic rules helps kick-start the process.

1. FORGIVE YOURSELF AND SILENCE THE VOICE OF THE CRITIC

Prior to our journey, it is essential that we forgive ourselves for our past failures and shortcomings. We have all messed up at some point. It is impossible to create profound change without leaving the past where it belongs, acknowledging our previous mistakes, failings and immaturity as necessary steps in the journey that brought us to where we are now. Partnered with that is the need to silence the internal critic that we imagine (and only imagine) haunts our progress and judges our actions. This voice is no more real than fairies and dragons were to Don Quixote. Who we were when we were children does not dictate who we are today. Our failings on previous jobs have no fix on our ability to perform our jobs in the future. We are never trapped in old paradigms unless we give them power and bring them into the present.

2. CONDUCT HONEST SELF-EVALUATIONS

While the internal critic should be banished since it is rarely fair and always cruel, in its place needs to enter the "fair assessor." This voice or perspective allows us to take a truly objective look at our own skills, attitudes and abilities in order to fairly, and with compassion for our own selves, identify our true strengths and weaknesses. It is okay to be harsh, but only if that is a fair assessment that any reasonable, healthy individual would give. It is also okay to be confident, but only within a realistic framework. Most of us suffer from one of two afflictions, both of which stem from a lack of self-awareness. The first is an inflated sense of ability, which is our ego speaking. The second, deflation, results in timidity and fear – which is also the ego – yet this time seeking to protect itself from further damage and embarrassment. A self-opinion that is skewed too far in either direction can paralyze the individual and stunt true growth and limit our effectiveness as change agents, whereas an objective view through a more detached self-analysis can have extraordinary results. Realistic assessments result in greater success and growth.

This self-analysis is an extremely difficult step for many to take, as it requires viewing yourself from the outside in and recognizing that the ego is not you. You have to detach yourself from your own ego as if you were giving your best friend advice.

A long-time friend of mine suffered terribly from an unhealthy body image that led to a serious eating disorder. Anorexia, bulimia and other eating disorders are extreme outward manifestations of unhealthy personal assessments. For her it meant that her own internal "measurement scale" had gotten completely off-balance. Unable to even correctly assess her physical form and weight, she was also unable to effectively see her potential, her intellect and her powerful talents. What she saw was someone with little value and who could not measure up. A long road of counseling helped her re-align her ability to conduct honest self-evaluations – and with it, her ability to contribute to community and family increased exponentially. While thankfully most of us do not suffer from these afflictions, more subtle versions are at work with our minds all the time – starving our true growth and potential.

3. ENVISION THE FUTURE YOU

Once it is possible to perform truly honest self-appraisals, it is now possible to set realistic and powerful goals that build upon your strengths and to begin your migration. What would you like to learn? What would you like to accomplish? What is your greatest ambition? What is your end game? What is the change you wish to affect?

With these goals in mind, then focus on the "you" that will be as you achieve your goals. How do you operate? How do you treat yourself and others? What do you feel? Feel this future you now. Be this person now!

Listen first to your instincts, and then to your rational mind and only then to the input of those around you. While many people do not know themselves very well, no one has the potential to know you better than you. What others say you can not do has absolutely no bearing on what you can and should attempt. Conversely, what you believe you can achieve has all the bearing in the world. Be the person that meets your goals. It is impossible to make progress without a vision for how you fit into that progress. Only by envisioning our hopes for the future can we build a path to get ourselves there.

SELF-PROJECTION AS A TOOL FOR CHANGE

"To be pleased with one's limits is a wretched state."
—Goethe

In the last couple of years of my undergraduate program, I met and fell in love with a wonderful but complex woman who taught me a lot about love and commitment and, ultimately, loss. For two years, we were inseparable and we developed a very strong friendship. But the relationship, like many college romances, was not to last. When she graduated, it became clear that she wanted different things than I did, and when she left and moved away I felt completely lost – gutted and heartbroken – having just lost my best friend and the person who featured prominently in all of the assumptions I had made for my future. In fact, the time was made even more difficult precisely because I had fallen in love with the "idea" of our life together and mourned also for the loss of that imagined reality.

During the last year of this relationship (my senior year), I began meeting weekly with a favorite professor of mine to discuss ideas, books and sustainability. I came to regard him as more than a mentor; I sought his advice and counsel on issues that extended far beyond the classroom. We became friends and collaborators. That said, I had never before discussed my relationship with my girlfriend with him until the week after my breakup. It had always seemed too personal and outside the bounds of our relationship.

Yet, unlike in previous meetings, I was completely unable to concentrate on anything we were planning to discuss – anything besides my personal suffering, which had taken on a larger-than-life significance to me. Looking back I was quite self-absorbed and feeling like the victim of life's cruelest lessons.

Easily seeing my distraction, my professor asked me what was the matter. And for the next several minutes without stopping to breathe, I explained what had happened and described what I was going through. He sat patiently and listened as I continued to describe feelings that I thought were very significant. I was feeling sorry for myself and I naturally expected him to commiserate with me and to offer consoling words.

Instead, he said, very matter-of-factly, "I'm sorry you feel this way, Jason. But what you are describing is in the past, not in the now.

And much of what you seem to mourn are the ideas you created out of your desired perception of the future. Those are also not in the now. Neither of those things can have any hold on you without your permission. I suggest that you come back to the now."

His reaction was not what I expected. His tone was neither harsh nor overly compassionate. It was simply the truth as he saw it.

Admittedly, at first I was shocked, then a bit angry, although I did not express it at the time. Normally when you share something sad people feel compelled to reflect back at you those same emotions – to enable you to continue feeling the way you are feeling. To validate. Rarely does someone from a position of caring tell you the truth of what you are experiencing.

At the time I could not understand how he could be so insensitive and react in a way that seemed to completely dismiss my feelings! I ended the meeting quickly thereafter and continued fuming as I walked across the campus. While his clarity stung they stuck with me and with those words echoing in my head I began to heal. It was some weeks later that I realized that he was, in fact, correct.

I was being self-indulgent and actually increasing my own pain by wallowing in the past as if it had been robbed from me and grieving an unattainable future that did not even exist. What I had lost was a close friend and lover in the now. The past memories could not be stolen and the future that did not exist could not be grieved. It was only the now that mattered. And I could deal with the now. Hour to hour, day to day it got easier. As I began to think of it that way, I found myself healing more and more quickly.

The experience taught me a powerful lesson about how our perceptions and expectations have the ability to alter our current realities. When we are sad we tend to become melodramatic and our ego fabricates stories of past and future to solidify our roles as victims, instead of facing the truth presented in the now — the real truth of the present.

Yet knowing how "real" our thoughts can be — how we can make ourselves happy or sad or angry simply by thinking certain thoughts — it becomes far more powerful to project a positive outcome and to "be the change we wish to see"[1] in the here and now.

In one of my last meetings with the professor I previously spoke of I talked to him again about his philosophy of being the change we seek in the now. He revealed to me how he used this approach to transform a certain component of his department at the university. Early in his tenure as a professor, he began to notice both opportunities and challenges within the system. Once he identified an unmet need, he "projected" what he personally wanted to do to help with the issue at hand. He worked hard to become the missing link or resource in the faculty. Regardless of where he started in the knowledge curve, through clarity of where he wanted to end up, he worked hard to amass enough expertise to eventually end up solving the challenge as he set out to do.

In the late 1980s he watched as computer applications gradually replaced manual drafting systems, and he became concerned when there was no indication that the university was preparing students for this inevitability as they entered the workforce. So he decided to become the department's internal computer expert, teaching himself what he needed to know and making no secret of his pursuit. As he "projected" or "became" the in-house specialist, students and faculty began to see him through that lens. His studies continued and he expanded his knowledge until he fulfilled his own prophecy. Rather

---

[1] To paraphrase Mahatma Gandhi

than acting externally as something he was not (he never overstated what he knew or falsely represented his knowledge), he internalized a self-projection until it became reality. He gave himself permission to broaden his area of expertise because he did not limit himself with negative self-talk about what he did not know or could not learn.

Under his leadership, the department soon brought on a full-time faculty member to oversee its computer curriculum, freeing him to turn his attention to other academic needs. He reinvented himself as one of the internal environmental experts (Oregon was blessed with several key figures in this area during my time there), steering students toward these critical issues in ways previously untaught.

To be very clear, what I call "self-projection" is very different than pretending to be what you are not. It is neither bragging nor lying; it is all about honest self-appraisal that helps us shed the shackles of insecurity. It is about having the courage to take a step forward into a future possibility with an openness to learning. Working "in the now" means focusing on what needs to be done in order to create the future we desire. In other words, self-projection means acting now like the person we want to be in the future, without ever claiming knowledge outside of our own limitations.

A STRONGER SELF, A GREENER WORLD

"It is never too late to become what you might have been."
—George Eliot

"What we vividly imagine, ardently desire, enthusiastically act upon must inevitably come to pass."
—Colin P. Sisson

There would be no point to a personal zugunruhe if one did not actually begin the actual migration. All that preparation needs to lead to something. And once you have mastered the idea of self-projection – and you are clear about the goals that you want to achieve and have honestly assessed where you are today — you are now ready to begin.

Beginning means being able to recognizes, sometimes subconsciously, opportunities that come up that allow you to move forward towards the goals of change you have set. But without first working on this type of self-projection, there is no context in which to make decisions or to determine if it will lead you in a positive direction. In other words, without a clear sense of a potential end-game in mind, a destination, it is impossible to know whether an opportunity will move you forward, backwards or merely sideways.

Projecting yourself into the future towards the truly sustainable future we desire means submitting to what your heart tells you is the right path. It sounds somewhat cliché. Yet, you must, in fact, believe in what is possible to get there. When our future goal is clear, it helps us focus our current efforts and avoid the inevitable distractions that come up. When we stay true to our own convictions through each and every decision, we become capable of so much more, regardless of how others perceive us. And our path forward is more likely to remain uncluttered.

In *The Power of Myth*, Joseph Campbell conveys this same idea as he discusses his powerful idea of following bliss:

> "Follow your bliss!
>
> Now, I came to this idea of bliss because in Sanskrit, which is the great spiritual language of the world, there are three terms that represent the brink, the jumping-off place to the ocean of

transcendence: sat-chit-ananda. The word 'Sat' means being. 'Chit' means consciousness. 'Ananda' means bliss or rapture. I thought, 'I don't know whether my consciousness is proper consciousness or not; I don't know whether what I know of my being is my proper being or not; but I do know where my rapture is. So let me hang on to rapture, and that will bring me both my consciousness and my being.' I think it worked."
—Joseph Campbell

So follow your bliss and now that you have a sense of the kind of change agent you wish to be, start the change that you feel urging you on. By envisioning the goal for ourselves and actualizing what it would be like to exist within that reality, we can back-cast from that place to make the process of change feel less daunting. Positive projection for the good of the planet is not only possible, it is imperative.

QUOTES TO CONSIDER

There are many wonderful words of wisdoms by great authors and thinkers who share this same philosophy. I leave you with a few to consider as you begin your journey.

You cannot transcend what you do not know. To go beyond yourself, you must know yourself.
—Sri Nisargadatta Maharaj

Change your thoughts and you change your world.
—Norman Vincent Peale

The greatest revolution of our generation is the discovery that human beings, by changing the inner attitudes of their minds, can change the outer aspects of their lives.
—William James

I can't change the direction of the wind. But I can adjust my sails.
—Unknown Author

Destiny is not a matter of chance, it is a matter of choice; it is not a thing to be waited for, it is a thing to be achieved.
—Winston Churchill

Times don't change. Men do.
—Sam Levenson

If you focus on result, you will never change. If you focus on change, you will get results.
—Jack Dixon

If you want things to be different, perhaps the answer is to become different yourself.
—Norman Vincent Peale

You cannot expect to achieve new goals or move beyond your present circumstances unless you change.
—Les Brown

Breaking the Tape

I believe there is no better example of the power of self-projection than the tale of Sir Roger Bannister, the British runner who broke records by breaking through perceptions of what is possible.

Until the middle of the 20th century, it was generally assumed that human beings were not capable of running a mile in less than four minutes. No one had ever done it, and even the most accomplished athletes fell short in their attempts. There was one man, however, who rejected the assumption that the species was unable to achieve such a milestone. Roger Bannister decided to train with that one goal in mind. He worked on the assumption that the four-minute mile was not only possible, but that he would be the man to make it happen. In spite of repeated failed attempts, he stayed true to his mission and to his unwavering belief. Sure enough, at a low-profile race in England in May 1954, Roger Bannister ran a mile in 3:59:40. By seeing himself as capable of something previously considered impossible, he elevated the entire sport.

What happened next is even more noteworthy: Roger Bannister only held the record for forty-six days. An Australian runner shaved another 1.5 seconds off of the time in June of that year, ushering in a wave of athletes and accomplishments that continue to wow the world and continue to break the record further. Today, runners in their 40s are coming in under four minutes. It is not as if the species has experienced a sudden evolutionary shift in how fast we are capable of running. The point is that we have shifted our perceptions of what is possible for our bodies to do.

Sports experts hail Sir Roger Bannister (who was knighted in 1975) as being responsible for one of the most significant milestones in athletic history, since his feat was about more than breaking a single record. Bannister demonstrated, through his drive and determination, that human potential is limited more by perception than by biology. When he broke the four-minute mile, it was a victory for those who reject the past as definitive and embrace the future as full of possibilities.

Imagine telling a migrating bird – "Sorry, there is no way you can fly several thousand miles – you are too small and weak. The weather conditions are too perilous and the dangers from predators too great. You must simply stay here and starve."

The bird, without our nagging self-doubts, imposed limitations and negative self-perceptions merely takes off, defying gravity and flies.

The migration begins – and one day soon she arrives at her destination.

G W E R S I   X

Learn to tell the truth to yourself as nobody has ever done.

Be neither too hard nor too soft, just realistic and optimistic.

Ask yourself how the most fair and wise judge would judge you, instead of the harsh critic or doubter.

Internalize this voice in your assessments and recognize the ego for what it is:

A false prophet within our heads.

GWERSI XI

What has been done is done; it is in the past,

Available for lessons, but not to be changed.

So do not dwell, but let go, forgive, move on, make amends, find peace,

As you can not go forward while staring backwards into the gloom.

GWERSI XII

You can not become something greater if you do not know where you are today or exactly where you should be when you arrive.

So set goals for your career, for your knowledge and for what you want to achieve.

Then project yourself into that reality and begin to act

(without taking yourself too seriously) like that reality is in the now.

Be both humble and confident, aware of what you know and do not know.

Be hungry to learn and change.

LOOKING FORWARD TO FAILURE:
LEARNING THE MOST WHEN THINGS GO WRONG

"An army of sheep led by a lion is better than an army
of lions led by a sheep."

—ALEXANDER THE GREAT

The phrase "Failure is not an option" has been attributed to Gene Kranz, the lead flight director for Houston-based Mission Control when directing NASA personnel on the ground to devise a method of saving the crew aboard the damaged Apollo 13 spacecraft in 1970. While these five words played great on the big screen when the true tale made its way to Hollywood, and they help to define a dramatic episode in American culture, the real story behind them, I would venture to guess, is far more complicated. In fact, I propose that what actually allowed the ground crew to succeed in this historically tense situation were their many failures that led to that moment. Because without failure – sometimes without repeated failures – there can be no context in which to place success.

We are taught in our culture that winners win and losers lose. It is a fairly black-and-white assessment and it is repeated often. It is particularly strong in the American (and to a lesser extent Canadian) mythos that we do not accept failure in ourselves or in others. Period.

However, anyone who has ever thought, "I'll never do/say/eat/build that again" knows the wisdom of making mistakes. How would we ever learn how to do things better if we denied ourselves the opportunity to do things badly? In this way, our failures help define us, perhaps even more powerfully than our victories.

Intellectually, this reasoning makes perfect sense. "If at first you don't succeed, try, try again," is repeated for good reason. But most of us still go to great lengths to avoid failure, primarily to protect our egos. Our sense of our own strength is tied to our internal track record of wins and losses. In addition, we become emotionally attached to our ideas and projects in a way that creates a personal sense of loss when things do not go well. So our affection for and attachment to our own work limits our ability to detach from it and allow it to fail, which in turn limits the very potential of the work.

From a young age, we are taught to take ourselves seriously. We learn that when we succeed – with our childhood milestones, at school, in relationships, in our careers – we are praised and rewarded. When one becomes an expert in a given subject, one is expected always to possess a certain wealth of information in that area – certainly not to fail! An expert always knows, and is not afforded the luxury of ignorance. When we are accustomed to success and taught that failures are "not an option," even small mistakes feel catastrophic. The reality, however, is that our moderate and sometimes large failures lead to our greatest accomplishments – if we let them.

Here is a cold, hard truth. If you are serious about being a change agent, you are going to fail – a lot. If you want to tackle challenging issues including cultural mores, regulatory hurdles, business paradigms or institutional frameworks, expect to lose a lot of battles. Failure is part of Zugunruhe. Expect it, welcome it, learn from it…then try again.

What is missing in our culture, and in the environmental movement to a large extent, is our willingness to thrust ourselves out there on that seemingly fragile limb where failure is likely to occur repeatedly. So we remain timid and stick to small, safe goals while every natural system on the planet is in a free fall. We would rather succeed and make little difference than fail trying to make significant change. Why? Because our egos can not take it! As previously discussed, we need to ditch this ego and step forward into change. We have lost the ability to be friends with failure, and this loss is very dangerous when you consider the size of the environmental and social obstacles we face. Constant feedback loops by learning what does and does not work is critical to being an effective green warrior.

A risk-averse culture usually finds itself on the decline. A risk-averse person rarely makes a difference. What is wonderful is to think that we were all born with the opposite tendencies. When a baby takes countless tumbles, testing the limits and discovering the abilities of her own physical self as she learns to walk, she is learning from and embracing failure. If we caught her every time she wobbled, she would never succeed independently. Great parents are those who understand that we can not overprotect and shelter our children. We must encourage them to take manageable risks and to learn from their own failures. We need to be there to pick them up and encourage them to try again. It is difficult to learn to ride a bike properly if mom never lets go of the seat.

Bob Berkebile tells a great story about how Buckminster Fuller once witnessed a mother jump across a room to stop her toddler from falling two feet off of a couch. Buckminster shouted out – "No! What a wonderful way for the child to learn about gravity!"

As professionals, we have too often internalized the risk-averse parent when we relegate our best ideas and greatest talents to the back shelf for fear of failure, and thereby stunt our own development. So many people with so much talent sit back and do nothing with it because they are afraid to fail. The sad irony with such thinking is that it tends to create a negative feedback loop, in which our timidity leads to mediocrity instead of excellence.

As the environmental movement gathers momentum and confronts a greatly impoverished world with seven billion people, we face a time of great transition and uncertainty. Humanity is in sore need of people who are willing to lead – and who are brave enough to fail by taking intelligent risks. We need people who are willing to speak out, to try new initiatives, to launch new business models and to reframe the way people think. Inevitably we need people who have the ability to embrace failures and to try again, now informed with more clarity about what does not work.

Buckminster Fuller and his students. Courtesy, The estate of R. Buckminster Fuller.

It is difficult to discuss revolutionary thinkers without returning to Buckminster Fuller who understood this concept perhaps like no other. When my mentor, Bob Berkebile, was a student at the University of Kansas in the late 1950s, Fuller served as a guest professor. His futuristic ideas about architecture and the environment seemed eccentric to many at the time, but his students were enthusiastic about his teachings and the great passion he displayed. Buckminster was a leader who believed that the "best way to make something obsolete was to invent its replacement".

In the class Berkebile attended, Fuller was deep into exploring his concept of "tensegrity", which was in its early phases. Fuller asked the students to design a large tensegrity structure based on the conceptual guidelines he provided. Over the course of a semester the group then worked together to build the various members of the structure, which they planned to assemble outside of campus in a much-anticipated public demonstration of the great Buckminster Fuller's revolutionary design concepts.

After weeks of hard work, the big day came, the group gathered and the audience watched as each student grabbed a piece of the giant form and slowly moved it backwards, bringing tension to play and allowing the structure to take shape and history to be made. Berkebile and his fellow students were exhilarated to be part of such a momentous event, and were proud of the contributions they had made both individually and as a class. With one final step, they provided the last bit of necessary tension and awaited the moment in which the tensegrity dome would fully erect itself. Instead, they watched in horror as one member buckled, and then the entire structure collapsed and fell apart in front of the watching crowd!

The experiment had failed. Their hard work was for nothing. They were devastated. Silence permeated the field.

And then...Buckminster's voice filled the vacuum.

"Yes, we've done it!," they heard Fuller exclaim in great joy.

The students were confused – what did he say?

Buckminster then gathered his dejected students around the pieces that lay on the ground, and enthusiastically praised them for a job well done.

He quickly pointed out to them that they had performed the most crucial experiment of all – they had uncovered the weakness in the structure and in his theory of tensegrity itself. Armed with this new, extremely valuable information, they could now make a bigger and better structure and rely more confidently on its success. They had found Fuller's own error. What a great day!

While the lesson was not intentional, it was infinitely more instructive – and some might say historic – than experiencing a flawless first attempt. Each student had learned the power of failure to teach and the attitude of a leader who embraces failure as a positive outcome. Where before the students felt personal ruin they now walked away shouting and cheering "Yes, we did it!"

That was 50 years ago, and Bob Berkebile still refers to this story as one of the most important lessons of his life.

While I was not lucky enough to study personally with Buckminster Fuller, I recall a less dramatic but still instructive academic experience of my own that provided wisdom on learning to sit with my own failures. In my first year of architecture school, I was given an assignment that most architecture and engineering students get – design and build a bridge and test it to the point of failure in front of the whole architecture school. There are many variations to this assignment, usually involving what materials are allowed in the construction and stipulations of how heavy and for how long a particular weight needs to be supported. In our case, the assignment was to build bridges out of wood, paper and cardboard only. We were not allowed to use any metal or other stronger materials.

The winning bridge would not merely be the strongest, but would, in fact, carry the most weight relative to its own weight. Understanding how to minimize the amount of unnecessary material was an important part of the assignment. Efficiency was key. As designers, we naturally wanted our bridges to look attractive as well. Like most students, I wanted my class bridge to stand out. Mine needed to be the strongest, the best looking and the most memorable – after all – everyone would be watching![1] I spent a great deal of time working on the design and "perfecting" how my bridge would go together. My partner and I looked at photos, sketched alternatives, calculated weight loads, gathered supplies and crafted a beautiful span.

As the day approached, we were excited and proud of the amazing structure we had built – our confidence was palpable. Unfortunately, the reality was quite the opposite. When it was our turn, the professor brought out the weights and starting with some very light loads, hooked them up to our bridge. Immediately the bridge began to sag to one side and then – bang – it collapsed in a spectacular explosion. It stood out all right, by failing almost immediately! We were mortified. Our only consolation was that we were not alone – many students had made the same mistakes we did.

The problem was that we were all so busy designing our bridges that we forgot to test them for the very properties that would ultimately make them fail. We were so confident that we did not allow for failure in the design process, a mistake that eventually led to a much bigger failure (a poor grade on the assignment).

The next year was very different. Learning from my mistakes (which surprisingly so many students did not do), I adjusted my strategy accordingly. The key lesson was that I needed to learn from failure.

---

[1] There's that pesky ego creeping in again.

So instead of spending all my time on the design and then hoping for success, I quickly built several bridges and tested them on my own until they failed. Each time I observed my error and quickly built another. I didn't worry about how the bridge looked – at least not right away... Dumping wood all together (which took longer to work with) my partner and I switched to cardboard and paper even though they were not as strong so that we could construct several test bridges in a fraction of the time that it took to build with wood. The day of the competition brought forth a bridge with multiple prototypes behind it. Some scoffed at our design – it had no wood! It was strange looking – looking frail in parts even! "This will be quick," someone said.

Yet we understood ahead of time where our bridge would fail and why — and we had a great understanding of how much weight it would carry. We sat back quietly and waited.

 And unlike the year before, pound after pound was added as people looked on with great surprise – a cardboard bridge that strong? It soon surpassed many of the wood structures. When it did fail, we cheered – knowing that in some small way we had changed our own paradigm of loss, failure and true success.

In my subsequent career, my failures have led me to my greatest moments. While I cannot say that I love to fail all the time, the lessons learned are never lost on me and I rarely take them to heart in a negative way for long. Sometimes I still become happy when something fails (and people think I am crazy).

I have been blessed to have had an amazing and successful career at such a young age, and people sometimes comment on how much I manage to get done successfully in such a short span of time. I usually just grin at them, as I know it is merely because I build a lot of bridges.

Like anyone, I actually have a fairly poor "hit rate" with ideas and initiatives. It is just that I have swung at a lot of pitches and when I miss I get right back in the batter's box immediately and adjust my stance or swing while others still ponder their next move. Eventually, I do hit the ball.

I would like to think that I now make fewer mistakes than I used to, but I rely on the fact that my many screw-ups have allowed me to find the path toward my own success. I force myself to be open to professionally vulnerable situations, I constantly "put myself out there", I refuse to perfect an idea prior to its release[2] and I fight the urge to retreat in the face of failure. I have found that the rewards are greater when I resist timidity. So it did not work – big deal. Try again.

Our greatest ideas are cultivated in the fertile ground of failed attempts properly mulched. Failure, then, is our most important teacher and has the power to lead us to magical moments.

Do you ever wonder at the amazing world we live in? At the millions of species of animals, plants, insects and microorganisms that live together on this great blue orb? And to learn that the vast majority of all species that have ever existed since life first emerged on this planet are extinct. Life has rewarded what works through constant experimentation.

Consider Bill Bryon's quote in *A Short History of Nearly Everything*, "The average species on Earth lasts for only about four million years, so if you wish to be around for billions of years, you must be as fickle as the atoms that made you. You must be prepared to change everything about yourself – shape, size, color, species affiliation, everything – and to do so repeatedly."

---

[2] A critical idea we will discuss in Chapter ¾ Baked.

GWERSI XIII

Look for opportunities to test yourself.

Be willing to fail, not just once but as many times as necessary.

For it is in the failure that true success is found.

Understanding why something works

Is best done through learning how and why it does not.

GWERSI XIV

When something does not go as originally planned,
embrace the change

And recognize that there is great value in having
assumptions and ideas proven wrong.

True growth comes from learning how to change

Rather than doing anything possible not to be wrong or to
keep things the same.

Only the fool views success as never having been wrong.

LEAD WITH LOVE AND BEAUTY:
ELEGANCE AND SPIRIT SHALL FOLLOW

"Your living is determined not so much by what life brings to you as by the attitude you bring to life; not so much by what happens to you as by the way your mind looks at what happens."

—KAHLIL GIBRAN

Words have great power, and they can mean so many things to different people when used in different contexts. Used improperly, words can create great rifts and conflicts and spread hatred and intolerance. Used with the right intention, words can heal, inspire and bring people together. Of all the words in the English language, I believe that there are four that have the most potential to become fulcrums for the positive change we seek:

BEAUTY ELEGANCE   SPIRIT AND **LOVE**

As stated in Corinthians 13:13, the greatest of these is love. If you think about what these four words mean, and imagine a world in which there is a continual abundance of reasons to use these words – a context that is worthy of their continued meaning – it is exhilarating. But if you then think of how often we actually get to use these words in describing our communities and our built environment, it is sobering indeed. While there are certainly pockets of beauty, elegance, spirit and love manifest in our society, the prevailing culture and inertia are more adequately described by words such as profit, growth, fear, efficiency and the mundane.

When you then extend this exercise to consider human relations, it becomes a bit easier to find examples that deserve their use. Yet too often people interact with each other in ways that are devoid of love and spirit. We are a narcissistic and selfish society much of the time. I submit that this is the fundamental reason why so much of the built environment – our suburbs and exurbs in particular, are created with so little beauty and elegance. Without a culture that nourishes relationships based on love and spirit, we are unable to design community infrastructure that supports it. Instead, we end up with miles of strip malls, billboards, big box retail and parking lots – temples to drive through indulgence, consumerism and efficiency.

Our communities, buildings and homes are outward manifestations of our relationships with each other, the wider community, the natural world and ourselves. There must be grace among us in order for there to be grace around us. It is our collective responsibility to seek solutions that are beautiful and filled with spirit – manifestations of great love and caring for the human condition and the rest of the natural world.

As we look to make significant changes in the world around us, it can be incredibly daunting, depressing and overwhelming. Simply watching the evening news or reading the headlines can be demoralizing, when so much energy is spent on vapid, meaningless tabloid content while society ignores critical issues such as poverty, climate change and war. In fighting for environmental change it is easy to get frustrated, angry, jaded and cynical and to simply play the role of critic, becoming a messenger of gloom and doom or shutting down. These are understandable and appropriate feelings to have when there is so much violence, ugliness and degradation apparent all around us. When you see environmental destruction such as mountain top removal in Appalachia, deforestation in the Amazon and mounds of toxic garbage from the industrialized world deposited in slums in India, it is hard not to respond with anger and frustration. These things should elicit strong responses from anyone with a pulse. But the real trick is to ask what we should do with that anger and frustration.

How do we act and communicate in order to become part of the change we wish to see? How do we deal appropriately with our feelings and channel our energy for positive outcomes?

I am reminded of how the Dalai Lama is known to giggle in the face of terrible events – something that makes some people uneasy at first. The Dalai Lama giggles not to ignore or make light of a grave situation, but because he is choosing deliberately to channel these emotions into tools of love and compassion. He is not giving his anger power, so that he can remain effective and present even under great duress.

It is a comfortable thing for me, someone trained in architecture and design, to discuss beauty and elegance as necessary parts of any solution. I have seen architecture lift people's spirits and literally change moods instantly in great structures. I understand what it means to create an elegant solution – one that just simply "works" without a lot of fuss and pretence (I also understand how hard it is). But I must admit that I feel self-conscious writing about incorporating love into everything we do – whether it is building design, business practices or relationships with institutions or organizations you wish to change.

Like many individuals, "love" is not a subject I am naturally comfortable discussing outside of private relationships. Having been raised in a left-brain-oriented, male-centered society, love and spirit is simply not discussed. Love is not rational, easily defined or quantifiable. And in our society something that can not be counted or quantifed is simply "squishy" or "fuzzy" and seen to have little importance in 'matters of consequence' to quote my favorite author.[1] There are those who believe that this is because we have so thoroughly discounted the feminine voice as a byproduct of the inequality afforded to women for so many centuries.

But what I know is profoundly true is this – just because something is difficult to quantify does not make it less real. In fact, the intangible and invisible can be more real and more important than things that are easily counted. There is, for example, a growing

---

[1] Antione De Saint Exupery

backlash among economists regarding the use of the GDP as a measure of a country's wealth since it does such a poor job at really measuring the things that truly matter to people within a country. The green architecture movement is finally waking up to the fact that beauty and design does matter in building performance, just as individuals who inhabit a building play the critical role in determining how a building is operated and maintained and whether it is reused or simply demolished at the end of its first life, all of which has everything to do with how much energy, water or other resources a given structure uses.

The truth is, anything meaningful and successful in the long term relies on love and compassion. In my experience, they are the most powerful tools in any relationship and, interestingly enough, also in any design. Love is actually the key, albeit a hidden component, to a truly integrated sustainable design. Love – for a place, for a community, for an ecosystem, for the people who will use a building – is what allows any project to transcend the ordinary to the profound. If we want a future that is ecologically healthy, socially just and aesthetically beautiful, then we must lead with love. Admit it – you are reading this book and starting your own Zugunruhe because you give a damn. You do it because you love.

BARRIERS TO CHANGE

The largest barriers to profound change are not technological or economic. Rather, they are people's attitudes, perceptions and fears and how we bring our own baggage into our relationships and into the work we do. We understand how "baggage" can influence relationships when thinking of romantic love, but we pay it little attention when we are discussing love of another kind. When groups of people start out with a real sense of partnership and respect –

professional love,[2] if you will – they can achieve incredible results. It is amazing, though, how many people who **would** see themselves as allies due to aligned visions and common goals, in fact treat each other instead with suspicion, jealousy, contempt and an unhealthy competitive sense. How many environmentalists and social justice practitioners spend time 'defending their turf' or 'putting other organizations in their place'. Many are so quick to judge and so slow to give the benefit of the doubt or to forgive people who, just like them, are trying to make a difference.

With our partners – our consultants, our clients, our employees, our competitors– we often have so little patience for the mistakes of others, yet we are indignant when someone points out our own oversights and short comings. We are so quick to write people off because someone "failed" in their attempt at something – when, as we already discussed failure is necessary. I have seen so many "green champions" make unhealthy assumptions about what others can and cannot do in order to limit that person's success or to feel better about their own achievements. The planet does not have time for its change agents to be so petty.

Change is extremely difficult for many of us to embrace. And yet, the most important change we can make is a change to the spirit of our relationships and dealings with others – even those we might see as competitors. Profound change – my definition of zugunruhe – requires that we empathize, extend a bit of ourselves, show compassion and express love, even to our fiercest opponents.

An important principle that I adhere to is this – forgiveness should happen prior to transgression. We all make mistakes. When it comes to environmental change we need to accept people where they

---

[2] C.S. Lewis described this love as philia or friendship love – the most admirable form because it involves no ego or passion as compared to romantic love.

are, in order to lead them gently to a place of higher potential. As we go forth to create change, we will meet with opposition at every turn. How do you react to this opposition? In anger? To be truly successful, we must act with love.

Out of all the chapters in this book, this one was the most difficult for me to write – the reason is that I too struggle with internalizing this lesson. When I am not centered and I am placed in a situation that is challenging, I tend to get defensive and to respond in ways that I hope will ensure that the conflict is resolved quickly to my satisfaction. However, what I have painfully observed is that when I react this way, there is typically some cost to the relationship or long-term situation that I am dealing with. Even when I win, I lose.

My wife is much better at the kind of understanding, patience and compassion for the other person's position than I am naturally, and I continually learn from her in this regard. It is one of the ways that we complement each other. I have learned that each time I extend love to someone in opposition to my objectives, the results are often magical. Not every time perhaps – but most of the time. This approach does not mean that I always get my way. Sometimes I do, but usually what results is a greater depth of understanding and new solutions or ideas emerge that result in a greater potential being realized down the line. In this way even when I lose, I win. Like anyone, when I am centered, I am effective. As you go forth, think on this concept. To be effective you must be centered. To be centered you must be acting from a place of love.

I recall words of wisdom spoken by Bob Mann, a mentor of mine who ran a successful Kansas City-based non-profit called Bridging the Gap. Bob always talked about the importance of accepting people where they are, and of the value of non-judgmental compassion. Standing first in someone else's proverbial shoes, he said, is the necessary first step on the path to change. It is always easier to work with the converted, or to criticize those of differing ideals. The real challenge, he taught, is to gain a deep understanding of what makes another individual think, and act, in a certain way. Bob's philosophy of empathy, of course, relies on heavy doses of leading with love. Wherever Bob went, elegant solutions soon followed.

LEAVING LOVE OUT OF IT

Early in my career, I served on a team for a large project that has stuck with me as an example of what can happen when there is a lack of love present among collaborators. My firm was brought in by a client to supplement the efforts of a local architect, since we were well known as one of the leading green firms in the country. Although the local designer was talented, he was labeled by the client as ill-equipped to handle the complicated green issues for which BNIM was nationally recognized. Unfortunately, the client was extremely insensitive in how he brought our team on board; rather than leading with love, he established an atmosphere that created some background tension and hostility.

In short, the client did not respect the local architect enough to trust him with the entire job. Perhaps this was a correct assessment. Yet, instead of focusing on the tremendous assets he did bring, the client made public remarks on his shortcomings and lack of expertise. The client's comments struck a chord with the man, and his confidence and authority weakened noticeably from that day forward. Our position, meanwhile, temporarily grew stronger, although a few of us on the BNIM team knew that the client was out of line and his actions made us uncomfortable as well. We failed to challenge his position and failed to consistently defend the skills of the local architect; by passively accepting the leadership role thrust upon us, we contributed to the project's toxic environment. We were flattered by the client's high regard for our team, but we did not do enough to repair the damage done by his insulting treatment of our professional colleague. Together, each of us contributed to an environment devoid of beauty, elegance, love and spirit. In the end, for a variety of reasons, not including the quality of the relationships involved, the project never got built.

THE GREEN EDGE

Designers and engineers are not supposed to get along – everyone knows that. There is a classic conflict between the supposed left-brain practical mindset of the engineer and the more right-brain conceptual thinking done by architects and artists. At least that is the stereotype; and while there is some truth to this perception, like any stereotype, it rarely is the whole truth.

For many years, I have collaborated with, Peter Rumsey, CEO of Rumsey Engineering, an engineer from Oakland, California. Flying in the face of the assumed acrimonious relationship between architects and engineers, Peter and I hit it off from the time we first met. We built a strong friendship as we gained mutual appreciation for each other's knowledge and work style. There has always been an unspoken understanding between us that when we sit down to work on a project together, we will begin by rolling up our sleeves and trying to solve the problems we both face. Our collaborative approach allows us to take the concept of integrated design to a higher level. Since we are always teaching each other, both of us are always in a state of learning. Since we are always combining our skills, we are always challenging each other to be better. Neither is afraid of asking seemingly naïve questions of the other, as the process always aids the project. Naturally, when we collaborate, problems arise as they do on any project. But even in tense moments, we face challenges as a team rather than from separate corners. Our mutual respect allows us to share our victories – as well as our failures.

For a couple of years Peter and I collaborated on a column for *Environmental Design and Construction Magazine* called The GreenEdge, where we used our different backgrounds to explore a wide range of green issues, including such topics as greenroofs and LEED AP status. Each year, we learned that it was the most read part of the magazine in reader surveys. I like to think that our deep respect for each other came through even in a simple magazine column.

RITA WALTHER-WITTENHEIM

No exploration of love from my perspective would be complete without mentioning my wonderful Aunt Rita, who taught me so much about relationships and injecting spirit into the things that I do. My aunt, my mother and all her sisters had an extremely challenging childhood, filled at times with incredible hardship and poverty. Strong family bonds helped them make it through these times – not always without tension, but always with support for each other. We used to spend parts of our summer with Aunt Rita at her small island cottage in northern Ontario that she and her family built by hand over a period of several years. We would swim, explore the island, catch frogs, climb rocks and build bridges. It was always a magical time filled with spirit and beauty that I will treasure for as long as I can remember. I attribute much of my love for the natural world to these summers.

One night, when I was older, on the last trip I ever made to the island[3], the two of us stayed up quite late while everyone else went to sleep.

---

[3] My aunt and uncle had to sell the island that summer due to their declining health.

We talked about many things – family, work, relationships – and we ended up in a discussion of the nature of love and commitment. The cabin had no electricity, only gas lamps and candles, and the mood was incredibly intimate and powerful under the glow of the kerosene flame. Near the end of our discussion, she leaned forward while smoking her hand-rolled cigarette (which was much more common in her generation) and said to me,

"Jason, I don't need anybody in this world...."

There was a huge pause and then,

"But I sure do want them."

She then went on and spoke to me about the difference between want and need, between desperation and appreciation and the power of relationships based on each person bringing something to the table as equals – not always in equal amounts and in equal ways – but in equal value. She spoke to me about Love through the wisdom of an elder who had seen her share of love and pain.

She asserted that it is far healthier to want than to need another. Needing someone, she said, implies smothering, possessing and controlling that person. From that place, we have a sense of entitlement, we take the relationship for granted and we are more likely to judge or disapprove.

Wanting another, on the other hand, allows us to approach the relationship from a place of strength and empathy. We are choosing to embrace or accept someone in. From here, we are more apt to listen and we are open to greater possibilities. In a non-romantic context, a relationship of mutual want is likely to be much more fruitful and productive as well. In the context of working to create a greener society, this rule carries significant weight.

She spoke about the need for inner strength and self-dependency as a requirement for reaching the highest levels of our own potential. Love for others must begin with love for oneself – not vanity and self-obsession, but an appreciation and honest appraisal of what you can and can not do – as we previously discussed. When you have inner strength and realize that you can do anything you need to for yourself while being at peace with it, then you are able to avoid being swayed by others or led down self-destructive paths. Perhaps more importantly, you are able to appreciate others for what they bring without attaching your own baggage to it; to truly appreciate people for the gifts that they have to share without being needy.

While I can not confess to always being able to operate in this mode, the memory of my Aunt Rita and the things she taught me continue to shape the way I think. As we move forward to create a new world, it is essential that we do so from a spirit of love, not anger; that we choose our partnerships, our alliances and our collaborators out of mutually beneficial want, not selfish need. If we only could do that, then the beauty, spirit and elegance we so desperately need to see would emerge in the work we do.

LEADING WITH LOVE – SOME RULES TO LIVE BY

- The first step in bringing about profound change is a change of attitude. Approaching a subject from a perspective of seeking beauty, elegance, love and spirit infuses the discussion with positive energy.

- Compassion and understanding are more effective motivators than guilt and shame.

- Once you can appreciate the issues, concerns, passions and expertise of others, you can celebrate them and put them to use for all concerned.

- Human attitude is a far greater barrier to profound change than technological or economic forces.

- It is more important to apply a good idea than it is to find and celebrate its origin. The best idea wins regardless of its author. Do not make achievements about you.

- There are bumps in the road on every project. Success is achieved when a group rallies to help an individual correct a mistake yet allows the individual to make mistakes.

- Draw lessons from those who may be more adept at discussing ideas – seek mentors and honor their wisdom.

- Do not be weakened by other people's poor treatment of you or your position. Stay true to your own convictions, even if those around you are not reacting as you would like.

- Treat yourself with kindness and respect, and you will bring the proper spirit to your relationships with others. Guilt and low self-esteem are the largest barriers to growth for any individual.

Let us look again at the idea of Leading with Love for Beauty, Elegance and Spirit, with quotes from my favorite author, Antoine De Saint Exupery:

BEAUTY

"What makes the desert beautiful is that somewhere it hides a well."

As human beings, we are naturally attracted to beauty. We seek it out in its various forms and respond to it on physical and emotional levels. Unfortunately, when it comes to the way we live our lives and the surroundings in which we place ourselves, we have begun to

accept a complete lack of beauty. Our built environment, including
the majority of the products we consume, is too often mass-produced
without regard to craftsmanship. The "Wal-Martization" of America
shows that our society has surrendered to this trend.

ELEGANCE

"Perfection is reached when nothing is left to be taken away."

Where we should have elegance, we have awkward solutions, clumsy
systems, huge mechanical processes and over-engineered packaging.
With a return to elegance, we have designs that function well without
being over-engineered. With over-design and mass production,
we lose that elegant perfection. When we build structures without
considering their environmental impact, or we accept over-packaging
as a necessary evil, or we forget to consider the connection between
ourselves and the products we consume, we abandon elegance.

LOVE

"For true love is inexhaustible: the more you give, the more you
have. And if you go to draw at the true fountainhead, the more
water you draw, the more abundant is its flow. Perhaps love is the
process of my leading you gently back to yourself."

In place of love, we are surrounded by violence, anger, apathy and fear,
and our built environments express these emotions. Our freeways,
barricades, blank façades and gated communities all serve as barriers
separating us from those around us. When we remove the walls and
make human connections, whether through personal, professional or
societal relationships, it has local and global effects. We must trust
and be trustworthy.

SPIRIT

"If you want to build a ship, don't drum up people to collect wood and don't assign them tasks and work, but rather teach them to long for the endless immensity of the sea."

Where there is no magic and no opportunity for discovery, there is no spirit. When designs and systems are presented in their most common forms, we rob ourselves of a unique journey. We strip our surroundings of any sense of wonder when all is revealed. Too many contemporary urban designs are bold and banal, and we exist in a world of flashing signs telling us what to do. The only way we will succeed in dealing with the huge shifts coming in the near-term – including peak oil and climate change – will be to fundamentally change the spirit we bring to our collaborations and innovations.

GWERSI XV

To create change requires leading with love.

Extend compassion and understanding as you work
with others

And have patience for things to unfold as they should.

Instead of judging, try supporting and you will be
amazed at the results.

GWERSI XVI

Working to help others and create change begins by helping yourself.

It is impossible to lead with love without loving yourself.

So treat yourself well and appreciate what you bring to the world,

Regardless of how small or large.

09

3/4 BAKED:
A RECIPE FOR SUCCESS

"The artist who aims at perfection in everything achieves it in nothing."

—EUGENE DELACROIX

AVOIDING THE CHASE FOR PERFECTION

As odd as it may sound, I have always tried not to seek perfection. Do not get me wrong; I always give my best effort and work extremely hard at whatever I do. I believe wholeheartedly in committing myself to each task I face, and devoting all of my knowledge and energy to the job at hand. I believe in excellence – just not "perfection".

One of the most important skills that anyone can learn regardless of the task or assignment, large or small, is knowing when to stop. I have spent a great deal of time working on recognizing the magical point at which any continued efforts might actually hinder a project's progress and diminish its potential; the magical point when it is time to release the work into the world to allow other individuals or forces to complete it.

This is the stage I refer to as ¾-baked.

When we refer to something as "half-baked," we often mean that it is inadequate or incomplete. The phrase has a negative implication. To extend the culinary metaphor, a half-baked item is undercooked; it is certainly unappetizing and it is possibly hazardous.

When I talk about ideas or tasks being ¾-baked, I mean that they have reached a special moment in time or development where the idea has significant shape, clarity and elegance. It can stand on its own, perfectly workable, yet still has room for some improvement, some rough edges and questions yet to be resolved. When a concept is ¾-baked, its original author or "architect" has taken it to a certain stage of near-completion, then, resisting the urge to keep refining, has offered it up to the outside world for feedback, criticism and testing. It is, so to speak, "taken out of the oven". Oddly enough, aiming for this stage of development and then sharing the work, rather than striving for perfection itself, is likely to bring about a more perfect result.

CONSIDER THE GOAL

From my perspective, when people strive to work on things to
the point of perfection, they are usually only fooling themselves.
"Perfectionists" spend so much time and energy making miniscule
improvements to whatever they are working on that they often end
up losing sight of the ultimate goals of the projects they tackle.
Typically the joy has been sucked out of the activity as well. We have
all heard the statistic that 90 percent of our efforts are expended on
10 percent of the result. It is usually the last 10 percent or the last 25
percent that does us in – and keeps good ideas from going somewhere.
Remember the earlier discussion of learning from failure…. The ¾
baked philosophy goes hand in hand with this maxim – putting your
ideas out in the world – even if they might fail.

When I studied in Glasgow, Scotland, I had a classmate who was an
incredibly talented designer. The only problem was that he always
aimed for perfection in everything he did. He would work endlessly
on something and never knew how to let go. He could not move on
until it was perfect, which meant that he rarely moved on at all.
He worked and worked and worked at things, never satisfied with
himself or his projects. He consistently produced beautiful artifacts,
but rarely completed them. Regardless of the assignment and its
importance, he put in the same amount of effort and placed the
same amount of pressure on himself. As a result, he suffered greatly
from stress, even over assignments that were inconsequential.
He had been carefully taught only to pursue perfection; indeed,
to equate his own value as a person with how close to perfect his
accomplishments were. Each assignment was a huge challenge for
this student – he did not know how to stop and be satisfied. Being
human, he repeatedly produced things that were less than perfect.
Not surprisingly, his self-esteem suffered greatly even though he was

brilliant. He had never learned the valuable lesson of scaling effort to the importance of the task at hand (if all you do is sprint, you never catch your breath). Nobody taught him that chasing perfection was a fool's errand and the harder he pursued it the further it got from his grasp. By the end of the year, my friend was close to failing due to the number of assignments that he simply could not complete. He refused to move on with one element of an assignment until it was perfect; then he ran out of time or became immobilized by the self-generated pressure. The sad thing was that the quality of his work was higher than just about anyone's in our year – but he was his own worst enemy. In trying to go for a home run each time, he never scored a single hit. As Edith Schaeffer notes,

"People throw away what they could have by insisting on perfection, which they cannot have, and looking for it where they will never find it."

Later in life, I became friends with a man who was an amazing trumpet player. From a young age, he showed talent that his father (as well as his teachers) spotted as real potential. In an effort to encourage his son, the father ended up instilling an unhealthy set of expectations focused on being "perfect." When my friend became older, he stopped playing altogether. I assumed that he quit because he no longer enjoyed the trumpet. In actuality, he told me that he loved the instrument and missed it terribly. But he gave it up when family and work obligations limited his practice time to what he perceived as an unacceptable level, and he began to hear nothing but his mistakes. For him, this artistic pursuit was all or nothing; he felt he needed to be perfect or not play at all. In his case, a quest for perfection killed the music in this man, and I believe that his life was less rich as a result.

One of the secrets to success is knowing when to stop, how hard to work and for how long. I have seen so many great talents waste their skills on the hubris of perfection.

"The greater the emphasis on perfection, the further it recedes."
—Haridas Chaudhuri

In so many disciplines, the "perfect is the enemy of the good." People obsess over details, worrying about acceptance, approval and propriety. By the time they do manage to finish an endeavor, the reality has often changed, making their deliberations all for naught. I have watched as skilled professionals have blown projects, not by underperforming, but by over-thinking to the point where they missed deadlines or exceeded budgets. Top athletes train to "peak" at certain times when it really matters. They have "off-seasons", and while they remain conditioned, they recognize that rising to the very top of their game is something that can only be done by spending the majority of their time not at the top of their game. All of us, regardless of the work we do, would be wise to remember this truism. Show me a perfectionist, and I will show you someone who does not get much done – unless they have learned to rein in these tendencies in a healthy way.

THE SWEET SPOT

"The thing that is really hard, and really amazing, is giving up on being perfect and beginning the work of becoming yourself."
—Anna Quindlen

How do we seek and identify the ¾-baked sweet spot of our own undertakings? How do we give ourselves permission to be less than perfect, while demanding from ourselves more than mediocrity?

Often, when I am seeking my own answers to life's dilemmas, I cook. I find that cooking provides many lessons applicable to our lives and the decisions we have to make. Releasing a project when it is ¾-baked is a lot like preparing asparagus. Let me explain:

If you steam fresh asparagus until it is "perfectly cooked," it will actually end up overdone and soggy by the time you eat it. Why? Because it continues to cook internally as long as it is hot. Anyone who enjoys this particular vegetable knows that there is a very fine line between deliciously al dente and horribly mushy asparagus. So often people wonder why it did not turn out right – "I took it out when it was perfect".

An experienced chef knows when to remove it from the hot water – while it is still undercooked; about ¾ cooked. Some even plunge it into cold water immediately after removing it from heat to slow the process further. In either case, it is the universe (metaphorically, in the form of cold water or the absence of hot water) that finishes the job to help accomplish crunchy-but-cooked excellence. The key to this metaphor is that you take the asparagus out of the water. You let it cool and serve it – and by the time it is ready to eat – well it just might be perfect...or darn close.

When we put something out in the world – an idea, a design, a project, even if great environmental importance is behind it – we must be willing to accept that the idea is not likely perfect despite our best efforts. When we are open to possible changes and criticisms and invite others to expand upon our original vision, we give our work and ourselves a great gift. When we hold onto an idea too long as we pursue its perfect execution, we run the risk of squeezing the life right out of it, missing relevancy from a timing perspective or never finishing.

So an idea's sweet spot – the time and place in which it is ¾-baked – is the point between its conception and its death by strangulation where there is the most potential for it to succeed. Crazy how it works – by letting the idea go before it is perfect, the likelihood of its success is greater. Fancy that.

IF YOU LOVE IT, SET IT FREE

When we release our ideas into world, incredible transformations can take place. It takes courage to let go of our biggest and boldest work (even our smallest ones), especially when doing so requires acknowledging imperfections and possibilities for error. But taking that chance often leads to great things – magical things even – when the ideas are good enough to take on a life of their own.

The universe has a way of providing what is required when we allow it to, doing away with bad ideas (usually for everyone's benefit) and elevating good ones.   The individual who gives birth to the idea, and is strong enough to release it fully when it is ¾-baked, enables the greater community to:

- Determine whether the idea is worthy

- Strengthen the idea and help it shine more brightly

- Focus importance on the idea rather than the author

- Find synergistic or complementary ideas

- Avoid potential pitfalls earlier with less time wasted

- Remind us all that letting go of our attachment to our ideas can be the best idea of all

After all, if it is change we seek, we need not concern ourselves with glory. Seeking perfection is really about assuaging the ego, more than it is about creating impact. If it is true impact that we seek, then releasing our ideas as often as we can is critical. Regardless, work released in the right spirit tends to find ways to reward its creator. The ideas that come out of the collective movement will safeguard our future, regardless of how or by whom they are created. Releasing ideas into the universe in the spirit of selfless passion for change results in powerful magic.

DO NOT RELEASE CRAP

All right, I still feel compelled to state the obvious. The ¾ baked philosophy is not an invitation to release shoddy, crappy work. The world is already full of half-baked ideas and poorly conceived projects. Do take the time to make your work clear, coherent, understandable at all times – worthy of sharing it with others. The more important the work, the more care that should be given. Is there a tension between not releasing crap and not trying to perfect something before releasing it? Absolutely. That is the whole point – the art of making effective change is learning to understand the idea of balance and quality...of beauty and elegance and how timing and effort relates to those ideas. You will not always get it right – but the first step is in understanding the tension, working hard – and then knowing when to stop.

The Living Building Challenge™ [1]

Since the mid-1990s, I have been focused on a concept that I call Living Buildings. I coined the term while working on a project in Montana called the EpiCenter[2], as our team sought to describe building performance that was "truly sustainable." The idea is that nature, not machines, provides the ideal metaphor and performance measuring stick for the buildings of the future – a vast departure from prevailing wisdom that viewed the "mechanistic world" as the icon of progress. The architect Le Corbusier famously said that "a house is a machine for living in" during the 1920s and summed up an attitude that has shaped architecture for the last century. For me, a paradigm shift occurred when Janine Benyus wrote her wonderful book *Biomimicry* –and although she did not address architecture in her book, she certainly opened my eyes to a different way of seeing the world.

What is a Living Building? Imagine a building designed and constructed to function as elegantly and efficiently as a flower; one that is informed specifically by place, climate, topography and microclimate. Imagine buildings that generate all their own energy with renewable resources; capture, treat and re-use water in a closed-loop process; operate pollution-free with no toxic chemicals used in any material – all while being

[1] For more information on the Living Building Challenge visit the International Living Building Institute – www.ilbi.org .

[2] The most advanced green building to never get built due to political issues at the University.

a beautiful inspiration to anyone who interacts with them. Even before LEED[3] came to fruition, Bob Berkebile and I spent hours focusing on how to develop the Living Building idea, eventually publishing a series of articles on the subject. Back in the late nineties, it was still a fuzzy concept – a vague notion of the kind of impact that we desired buildings to have even though we continued to talk about the idea to every client who would listen. "You need us to design you a living building," we would always say. In 2000, a BNIM-led interdisciplinary team did a substantial amount of research for the David and Lucile Packard Foundation[4] on what a living building would cost as compared to LEED and conventional construction.

In 2005, I was encouraged by the growing strides that the green building industry was finally making. I had worked on two Platinum LEED projects and three Gold LEED as well as other Silver and Certified projects, all of which were done on budget (or close) and on time, and I was convinced that the industry was ready to go deeper. So, in my spare time in the evenings and on weekends, I began writing the world's most stringent green building standard, for the first time, clearly codifying what a Living Building really needed to do to deserve the designation.

---

[3] LEED stands for Leadership in Energy and Environmental Design and is the most influential rating system in North America, designed and operated by the U.S. Green Building Council. For more information on LEED visit www.usgbc.org

[4] The result was the David and Lucile Packard Foundation Sustainability Matrix.

I finished the first version of the Living Building Challenge (LBC) while moving out to Seattle before starting as the new CEO of the Cascadia Region Green Building Council[5] in the summer of 2006. I knew that what I had on my hands was a very special document, but I also understood that it was far from perfect. It was a powerful idea – ¾-baked – and ready to be shared with the industry.

I decided to bring the intellectual property to Cascadia and to give it away without asking for any compensation. It had too much potential to be "owned" by a single individual, or any single architecture firm and the spirit of the tool demanded that personal profit could not be a motivator in releasing the work. So, in my very first board meeting with Cascadia — in what was a complete surprise to them — I made a presentation sharing the LBC and offered to give it to the non-government organization (NGO), but with one important condition: when I offered the tool to the organization's board of directors, I told them that they could have it, provided that we made it a centerpiece in the organization's future and that we would invest significant resources into its development and adoption. Without hesitation they adopted it in a unanimous vote and that single act of leadership has now led to a huge chain of powerful and positive outcomes that is helping to change the building industry, state and local laws and ordinances and the very way many architectural design firms design buildings.

[5] The word "Region" has since been dropped in the name of the organization. It is now simply the Cascadia Green Building Council.

Clockwise from top left. **1.** Xstrata Nickel Sustainable Energy Centre at Cambrian College; Sudbury, Ontario; Castellan James + Partners; **2.** Omega Center for Sustainable Living; Rhinebeck, New York; BNIM Architects; **3.** Hawaii Preparatory Academy Energy Lab; Kamuela, Hawaii; Flansburgh Architects; **4.** Center for Interactive Research on Sustainability; Vancouver, British Columbia; Busby Perkins + Will; **5.** Oregon Sustainability Center; Portland, Oregon; GBD/ṢERA Architects.

Any transformative idea needs three things to create widespread change: the right timing (timing is indeed everything), the right message artfully delivered and the right platform.

With Cascadia, all three finally began to align to make the Living Building Challenge a reality around North America and increasingly around the world. Pulling some strings with some friends at the U.S. Green Building Council, Bob Berkebile and I reunited to present the idea at the 2006 GreenBuild[6] in Denver to a crowd of several thousand leading practitioners. Opening right before my childhood hero, David Suzuki, we asked the assembled delegation to join us in accepting the "Challenge." In a moment that will always remain a powerful personal milestone for me, the whole assembly rose in a spontaneous standing ovation. Releasing a ¾-baked idea (for it was far from perfect) had started a paradigm shift in the building industry.[7]

Since then, what has happened has been truly phenomenal: dozens of projects have emerged all over North America and beyond, racing to be the first Living Buildings anywhere – the first of which may be certified by the time this book comes to print.

These buildings will provide critical models for how people will live, work and play in the coming decades, finally reconciling the balance between the natural and built environments. Thousands

[6] Greenbuild is the nation's leading green building conference held in a different major metropolitan area each year.

[7] To read much more on the Living Building Challenge and the huge changes it is motivating, visit www.ilbi.org.

of people from many different disciplines – most of whom I have never even met – are now working to advance the ideas of the Living Building Challenge in their communities. In late 2009 the 2.0 version of the LBC was released – based on continous feedback from dozens of practitioners helping us make the program stronger. Still far from perfect, we inch closer as a community, excited that the new version now encompasses all kinds of design and construction including renovations, infrastructure, and now whole neighborhood and community designs as well as addressing issues of social justice, equity, transportation and food production for the first time in a green building standard.

The Living Building Challenge is now operated by the International Living Building Institute (www.ilbi.org) with a collaboration in Canada with the Canada Green Building Council and chapter organizations in Ireland and Mexico.

GWERSI XVII

In any endeavor, scale the effort of your work to the effort required for success.

Accept that sometimes your "best" varies under different conditions.

Do not overthink or overdo.

Learning balance and restraint without harsh internal judgment is a fundamental requirement of true success.

Perfection comes not when it is sought, but when it is not.

GWERSI XVIII

Release your ideas and innovations to the world when they are 3/4-baked.

Learn when to stop and invite others to contribute and collaborate.

Reject the urge to constantly refine and improve until something is perfect before sharing.

Chasing perfection is a fool's errand.

The chance for perfection grows by letting go,

Not by hanging on.

10

CONFLICT AND THE FIGHT FOR PEACEFUL SUSTAINABILITY:
EMBRACING CONFLICT FOR TRUE GROWTH

"Those who practice the Art of Peace must protect the domain of Mother Nature, the divine reflection of creation, and keep it lovely and fresh. Warriorship gives birth to natural beauty. The subtle techniques of a warrior arise as naturally as the appearance of spring, summer, autumn, and winter. Warriorship is none other than the vitality that sustains all life."

—MORIHEI UESHIBA (INVENTOR OF AIKIDO)

EMBRACING AND ENGAGING CONFLICT

This much is true: change and conflict go hand in hand. Profound change relies on conflict, so if we are committed to the first, we must embrace the second.

But conflict, for many people, has only a negative connotation. By its very definition, it requires two parties to "come into collision" or to "clash." How, then, can we balance our commitments to peace and sustainability with a willingness to engage in conflict?

Creating profound change in other people, systems and cultures requires that we first take a long, hard look at what we think we know and understand. Thinking back to the first chapter, zugunruhe begins when we ask ourselves what we have become too comfortable with and what feels safe to us yet lies in conflict with the change we wish to seek and the person we wish to become. Only by manifesting profound inner change and beginning our own migration towards greater effectiveness and peace can we create positive outer change that is durable and beautiful. In essence, it is essential that we stir up conflict within ourselves as we begin the journey down the change-making path. Viewed this way, conflict can be seen as a vital and healthy part of any change – inward or outward.

Conflict, like failure, is necessary. Unfortunately, we tend to have an equally unhealthy and dysfunctional relationship with conflict just as we do with failure.

There are, unfortunately, always significant numbers of angry and hurt individuals who embrace conflict for extremely unhealthy reasons – as an outlet for their aggression, pain and confusion. Conflict in this setting is violent, intended to hurt and is pursued almost as a means to its own ends. This modus operandi is not what is meant by truly embracing conflict. Other people shy away from conflict at almost any cost, usually for one of the following two critical reasons:

FEAR. When we stay in situations that make us unhappy, it is usually because we are afraid of change and of the conflict change creates. Instead, we internalize it, trying to avoid the outer manifestation of conflict, which is somehow believed to be too scary or intense to deal with. Yet the "conflict" does not go away; it merely eats inward and builds. There are many people who, instead of engaging and speaking up for what is right or asking for something that they need, bottle up their emotions, internalize negative energy and end up sacrificing their own well-being and effectiveness. By not expressing ourselves when we disagree with a boss, co-worker, client, friend or lover, we actually own the opposing view as surely as if we had agreed with it in the first place. And then we resent ourselves and the other for our weakness.

Ironically, this fear of conflict ends up being dramatically self-fulfilling as, at some point, the internal conflict comes to the surface in destructive ways – inappropriate anger, yelling and sometimes violence. However, when we stand up for ourselves and our convictions in a respectful and positive manner – embracing the various forms of resulting conflict – we allow ourselves to grow and ultimately challenge others to do so as well.

INSECURITY. Many of us equate conflict with rage, and view all forms of conflict as personal attacks. People with deep insecurities feel hurt and wounded with every interaction where an issue or idea is challenged, as they too closely associate the notion of conflict with a feeling that they are personally defective or bad. They then feel victimized as any conflict persists and they reply only with pain and anger to defend what now feels like a personal attack. They have not learned that conflict is something that happens "out there" and has no internal purchase if it is not granted and that conflict can be healthy and isolated to a particular issue that needs to be aired, separate from personal feelings. By making conflict personal it only shuts down rather than opens-up discussion. By learning to clearly separate who we are, and our own value from whatever conflict that arises, we greatly increase our effectiveness.

Our goal, then, is to understand that conflict is necessary, important and healthy and find peace in conflict even when it is initially difficult and uncomfortable to do so.

CONFLICT VERSUS COMPETITION

I have learned that using conflict as a tool for change takes practice. The goal should never be simply to overpower an opponent; instead, conflict is put to most effective use when it is used to elevate the potential of those on all sides of an issue. In order to illustrate this point, I recall a literal experience from my childhood that serves as a good parable.

Growing up, I was a very skinny kid, a fact that led some of my peers to tease me and assume that they could push me around because of my slight build. I was encouraged by my father to take judo, so I could learn to defend myself if push came to shove, so to speak. Strictly translated, judo means "the gentle way". In judo, the objective is to use an opponent's energy and inertia against him. One achieves this end by throwing and pinning, not by striking or intentionally causing physical pain. A highly skilled practitioner marks success by preventing both injury and damage to the attacker, while stopping his or her opponent from hurting them.

I took to judo with great interest, joining two other friends in a local dojo and practicing hard each week. I studied regularly over the course of several years and actually developed decent skills; the sport came naturally to me and I enjoyed participating in tournaments that my father took me to all over northern Ontario. Looking back, I think I was good at judo because I could anticipate the moves other children were preparing to make[1], which allowed me to beat them even when they were stronger and faster than I. I had success beating other judoists who had higher belts and better technique. I understood how to win.

Unfortunately, in retrospect I was not necessarily learning the discipline I should have been. Like some others, I did not study and memorize Japanese terminology for the throws I was learning – and I did not spend sufficient time practicing proper technique. I was concerned only if a move worked. I think my Sensei understood this, but because I was doing well in tournaments against higher-ranked opponents, I think he felt compelled to promote me when he should not have. Perhaps he should have insisted on more discipline, since the goal is never simply to win.

I learned this lesson painfully one winter afternoon in Timmins, Ontario when I faced a young boy approximately my age from a neighboring town. He was one degree higher than I was in rank and a worthy opponent. But I had a trick up my sleeve. I had been observing older, considerably more advanced students and had studied a particular "counter"[2] that looked extremely interesting. I had seen it used in a recent match that resulted in an immediate "ippon" (full point) and figured that I should try it as well. It was not a throw that I had ever practiced or been properly taught – but I knew

---

[1] I was always surprised at how so many essentially "telegraphed" their intended moves and tried to rely only on their strength or some sort of practiced sequence to fight.

[2] A counter is a move designed specifically to be used to stop or turn the tables on your opponent's move.

I could win with it. My cleverness, I thought, would make up for my lack of higher belt mastery.

In the early moments of the match, I worked hard to mislead my opponent with fake attempts at throws (a technique I often used). The goal was to make it seem like I was vulnerable and to reveal how he approached his throws. I quickly learned that if I pulled him a bit to the right after tugging him extremely hard downwards, he was prone to try a particular type of leg sweep in response. I simply had to watch for his sweeping right leg; if I was not careful, that leg would throw me to the ground and he would gain a point. After a few minutes of us sparring in this way, I was ready to try my experiment. I planned to put myself in the position of the victim and at the last minute when he was about to throw me, I would hook his leg and flip him back over me as I had seen the black-belts do.

The right moment came, and I tugged hard downwards to the left, then pulled him back up to the right, feigning a lack of balance. He swept his leg forward with confidence and using all his strength. And then I did almost exactly what I had seen the older students do: I sent him soaring over me in a complete somersault. He landed flat on his back in an instant full-point victory for me. "Ippon!" But what I had not done, what I had not known how to do, was to protect him at the same time. He was not my adversary, but my collaborator whom I let down. And as he came down on his back, he did so with his leg bent completely downward in the wrong direction. Upon impact, his leg snapped in two places.

As I stood up, he started screaming and crying and thrashing about on the floor and I was horrified. The ceremonial rules of the sport meant that I had to sit on the mat with my back to him listening to him scream until he could be removed from the mat by the ambulance. It was a long few minutes and gave me a new perspective that I will never forget. I wanted to win the conflict instead of using the conflict to better my own development. The cost of this victory was too high.

The experience took most of the fun out of the sport for me from that point on. The injured boy never returned to judo, and I learned a hard but extremely important lesson about conflict. The match taught me that conflict in any form – physical, mental, spiritual – is an art that requires practice to master. Just as I was unwilling to practice in order to win that important contest, our society has become lazy and unwilling to engage in productive conflict because it often seems too difficult. Either we avoid conflict or we take shortcuts to try to get the result we want. In true conflict, we have partners with whom we collaborate rather than spar. Together, both sides of a conflict can redirect energy in productive ways to the satisfaction of all concerned.

CONFLICT AND THE GREEN WARRIOR

Some people have asked me why I use the term "warrior" when I describe individuals who quest for profound change. Many feel that the term brings a negative and violent connotation. And, while I understand this to be the modern western view of the term, I believe the reverse is actually historically true. In many past cultures, a true "warrior" was someone who possessed great discipline; a warrior considered bloodshed and violence to be unnecessary in almost any situation and always undesirable, never cold-blooded and pre-emptive. Restraint and diplomacy were the hallmarks of a great warrior. A warrior was willing and able to fight to be sure, but as a measure of last resort.

I now use the term "green warrior" as a metaphor. In *Zen and the Art of Making a Living*, author Laurence G. Boldt describes a warrior as "anyone who uses their aggressive energy in a disciplined, focused way." He reminds us that even Gandhi understood the power of focused aggressive energy:

"I have learned through bitter experience the one supreme lesson to conserve my anger, and as heat conserved is transmuted into energy, even so anger controlled can be transmuted into an energy which can move the world."
—Mahatma Gandhi

The environmental issues we face today should make us angry. They should make us unsettled and outraged, and should drive us to true warriorship – not cowardly acts of ecoterrorism, but profound and sustained lifelong dedication to transformation. The question, when anger rises, is not whether the feeling is legitimate – it probably is – but what is the most effective way to deal with these feelings and how one can channel such energy towards conflict that is productive.

The green warrior takes responsibility by controlling her outrage and channeling it into effective action. As green warriors, we do not seek to destroy those who stand in the way of progress, but instead use their negative energy and convert it to positive change and a new paradigm, including for those that we are up against. Warriors use dialogue, imagery and vision to convert others' negative worldviews to more holistic, encompassing and sustainable perspectives. To use judo again, we are willing to "throw" people and make them submit... but we refuse to break bones and win at a cost that is too high.

David Bohm[3] distinguishes the word "discussion" from "dialogue," masterfully illustrating the difference between effective and ineffective conflict:

---

[3] From his book *On Dialogue*

It has to do with the words "dialogue" and "discussion." The word "dialogue" comes from the Greek "dia-logos". "Logos" means meaning or word. "Dia" means through. The original meaning of the word "dia-logos" was meaning moves through or flow of meaning. When a group of people talk with one another so that there is a flow of meaning, this is a very special kind of conversation. We become unconcerned about who says what, about whose view prevails or who saves face. We enter the domain of truly thinking together. By contrast, the word "discussion" comes from the same roots as "percussion" and "concussion". It literally means, "to break apart." A discussion involves heaving one's views at one another. Who wins and who loses is often all that matters.

Serving as a true green warrior requires that one embrace and accept conflict, and approach it as a necessary tool for change.

Toward this end, the practice that we need is the following:

- The willingness to risk getting hurt or risk being wrong

- The courage to potentially upset and provoke people we care about

- The patience to listen to what others are saying

- The humility to accept when we are wrong

- The clarity to convey how we truly feel

- The wisdom to explore new points of view and accept other positions

- The love to see each conflict through to a higher resolution[4]

In the current green building movement, there is a small but growing number of extremely dedicated and passionate green warriors, each

---

[4] There is that wonderful and well-known prayer by Reinhold Niebuhr that is filled with meaning: "God grant me the serenity to accept the things I cannot change; courage to change the things I can; and wisdom to know the difference."

willing and prepared to engage in productive conflict. Unfortunately, this number is just not enough. In order to make real and effective change on the necessary scale, we need a massive army of well-trained, highly skilled green warriors who are driven by positive-focused motivations. The environmental movement has produced a substantial number of advocates, but many are misguided, uneducated and ineffective, in spite of their intelligence. Some are simply pissed off and unpleasant.

The green warrior must be ready before going into action. Too many of us are ill prepared; we do not understand the idea of treating those we conflict with as a "partner." When dealing with institutions or individuals we seek to change, we lack a clear strategy and we have not suitably honed our skills to have a hope of succeeding beyond further polarizations.

PEARLS OF WISDOM

In any conflict, we must think of the person or position we attempt to change as a partner rather than an enemy. Armed with knowledge, passion and a willingness to engage, we move debates forward constructively. I have always admired the teachings of Thomas Crum, John Denver's old bodyguard and a skilled black belt in aikido (a martial art similar in form and philosophy to judo). In aikido, the Uke and Nage[5] work together as peaceful opponents to master technique. In Crum's work, he often uses aikido as a metaphor for change and for accepting and embracing conflict as an essential part of that change.

In his book *The Magic of Conflict*, Crum reminds us that the goal of conflict is not to bring people to your side, but to bring them to

---

[5] Uke is the receiver who initially starts an "attack." The Nage defends and gracefully performs the throw or move on the attacker. Both Uke and Nage take turns and help each other with form and movement.

something larger than either side. He explores the notion of conflict as being neither positive nor negative; it is nothing more than an interface pattern of natural energies. Crum cites beaches, canyons, mountains and pearls as perfect examples of how nature uses conflict as its primary motivator for change.

Further jewels from Crum's work, which summarize the potential power of conflict:

- We all have conflict in our lives; it is unavoidable. It is what you do with that conflict that makes a difference.

- Conflict is not a contest. The goal is not to win or lose; it is to learn, grow and cooperate.

- Conflict can be seen as a gift of energy, in which neither side loses and a new dance is created.

- Resolving conflict is rarely about who is right. It is about acknowledging and appreciating differences.

- Conflict begins within. As we unhitch the burden of belief systems and heighten our perceptions, we love more fully and freely.

- Understand and embrace conflict and aggression.

- Conflict starts with knowledge.

- We must know our opponent's opinions in order to engage her with skill and empathy.

It is necessary to work directly with the conflict in our environment, not ignore it, submerge it, give up on it or try to deny its existence. However profound our individual wisdom, it will not survive unless it is joined with some kind of power.

GWERSI XIX

Embrace conflict as a necessary and valuable part of change.

Do not avoid it, hide from it or seek it recklessly, but step into it when necessary.

Use conflict as inertia in which to move from one paradigm to another.

G W E R S I   X X

Do not view conflict as an opportunity to win or defeat an opponent.

Instead, view it as an opportunity to test mutual assumptions, ideas and policies,

Arriving at a place that is healthier, more profound and more true.

11

BACKING GUTS WITH MEASUREMENT:
FROM RULES OF THUMB TO RIGHT-SIZED REALITY

"In God we trust. All others bring data."

—PETER RUMSEY

I have long been a fan of the book *Your Money or Your Life* by Joe Dominguez and Vicki Robin because it offers a simple program of measuring personal spending that, if followed, can really have an impact on people's lives. The exercise involves logging all purchases made in a single day, no matter how small, for a period of a month as a way of revealing the cumulative expense of seemingly innocuous habits. We have all heard the reminder that if we resist the urge to splurge on a daily three-dollar latte, we can save more than a thousand dollars in a single year. It is all a simple matter of measurement – and, of course, discipline. Our little habits have a way of adding up.

Applying this same principle to our desire to live greener lives, we must ask ourselves important measurement-related questions in order to understand our own patterns. How much energy do we use in our homes How much solid refuse do we generate on a monthly basis? How many gallons of gasoline do we purchase each week? If we have not stopped to measure our own usage or those of our businesses in these easily quantifiable categories, how do we expect to know how we, as individuals, can affect change on a grander scale?

Far too often, consumers and professionals make assumptions without questioning the fundamentals on which they are based. For example, we assume that certain problem-solving approaches work best because they are the ones we have always used. We manage our finances, organize our clutter and construct our built environment in the same manner, year after year. Why change habits that seem to be working? The point, though, is that we do not often stop to examine how well our daily habits actually work. Which means that we do not truly understand our own behaviors. Something that is not failing is not the same thing as something that is optimized. Just because something has not failed does not mean it is truly working. One thing that is for certain – you can not change what you do not understand, and you can not understand something until you measure it in some way.

Throughout this book I give the advice to "follow instinct, to trust your gut as it were". But this does not mean that you throw out logical, rationale analysis. A powerful change agent has many tools at her arsenal. You can go on "gut" for certain things, but if you seek a deeply green existence (or profession), then you must also learn when measuring, testing and analyzing reveals new powerful insights. You must look more scientifically at your own patterns, tracking data over long stretches, in order to reveal meaningful trends. In other words, you must back your intuition with measurement and it is amazing how the two sets of tools – right and left brain – can be powerful complements.

GAINING AWARENESS

"The fruits of philosophy (are the important thing), not the philosophy itself. When we ask the time, we don't want to know how watches are constructed."
—Georg Christoph Lichtenberg

In the early days of my architecture career, I was amazed at the ways in which so many critically important decisions were made. A large percentage of the professionals I came across – contractors, architects – yes even engineers – representing all spectrums of the building profession – made many of their decisions based simply on "how we did it last time" or (perhaps worst of all) "rules of thumb". These decisions were made according to what had seemed to work in the past, with very little concern for testing and analysis. I was dismayed by a real lack of intellectual rigor that would seem to demand that people actually test their assumptions, check their calculations or do some sort of post-occupancy evaluation. But sadly, as soon as a project was done it was "gone". Habit and "standard procedures" dictated most of what was done and, unless there was a significant failure of some type, it was not changed. New materials, systems or approaches were resisted (like many aspects of green design) simply because they had not been used before, and the risk of stepping outside of what was comfortable was a problem.

In my estimation, "not failing" is quite different from succeeding. Observing such patterns made me want to explore whether these solutions were producing optimal results. Were objectives really being met? Just because someone did not sue you, did that mean it was successful? Could we, in fact, do better? What were the real environmental impacts of the works? Were the projects making people happy and/or healthy or was the work merely satisfactory? Was it possible to measure these desired outcomes?

Those not in the building professions are often surprised that it is actually quite rare for an architect, engineer or contractor to return to a previous design or project and actually measure the job's performance beyond anecdotal feedback. Imagine designing a $100 million building and then never really going back to determine if the occupants like working there? Or if something you thought was critically important to the design actually performed as intended? It seems shocking, but less than 5 percent of large commercial projects[1] receive any kind of post-occupancy evaluation to determine how design, engineering and construction decisions have been successful. A large percentage of those that are measured are done so simply because there is something terribly wrong with the building – sick building syndrome, leaking or structural failure. It is amazing with something so important that so little analysis is performed. Imagine if the aeronautical or automotive industries took that approach! Unless there is a lawsuit, there is rarely a feedback loop when it comes to buildings.

---

[1] From the American Institute of Architects (AIA)

The problem rests not only with the building professionals – building owners are equally culpable and usually do not want to spend any money to have their building tested or even "tuned" after some period of time. Post-occupancy evaluations are rarely funded and studies that do exist are typically looking only at a few issues due to time and fiscal restraints. How can designs evolve without any feedback?

Moving from buildings to people and institutions, how can any of us evolve without similar feedback? How often do we truly analyze and measure how we work?

RIGHTSIZING

Let us continue using the building universe as a metaphor for the discussion of measurements.

The engineering world is in a prime position to affect profound environmental change, yet it is rife with disturbing examples of missed potential and wasted energy and resources. When I worked in Kansas City, for example, I was shocked at how grossly oversized so many buildings' mechanical systems were. In some cases, brand new mechanical systems were four or five times larger than what was necessary to meet an individual structure's true demands. In fact, many were so grossly oversized that it was physically impossible to ever meet the demand that was the basis for the design. Some amount of over-sizing, known as "redundancy," is prudent in any engineering solution in order to allow for extreme conditions that occur. But too much redundancy results in significant waste and inefficiency.

When large building equipment such as chillers and cooling towers run only on partial loads, the equipment runs very inefficiently as they were not designed to work well on "partial loading" and significant money and environmental resources get wasted simply because the system is not optimized. Significant funds are also wasted upfront when such huge equipment is purchased in place of smaller more cost-effective systems appropriate to the true load.

I have seen more than one example where hundreds of thousands of upfront dollars were wasted on oversized mechanical systems simply to make the engineer of record "comfortable" that capacity would always exist. In essence, these engineers were using their clients' money to give them an insurance policy that exceeded their total fee for the project in the first place. Shameful really, especially when that money could have been put to better use improving the building in other ways.

In my estimation, the engineers on these projects simply did not make the effort to measure how their previously designed buildings were actually used. Instead, they relied on outdated rules of thumb and "common practice" to determine their results. In most cases, the engineers were being paid for sufficiency, not efficiency, and their fees were often tied to the size of the mechanical systems installed, providing a perverse disincentive to rightsizing a system – especially if their fees were low to begin with. Why would anyone want to take risk when they were underpaid and the incentives encourage the opposite behavior? As long as nobody complained too much, then things never changed.

One project in particular stands out. While at BNIM, I was brought in as a consultant to help "green" an existing design for a large "Class A"[2] commercial office building heavily dependant on its mechanical systems. Given the mechanical systems involved, I sent for backup in the form of my frequent collaborator and mentor, Ron Perkins, a genius mechanical engineer from Houston, Texas. Ron differed from

---

[2] Class A office means what it sounds like – it refers to "best in class" office space for a given market in terms of features and quality, commanding the top end of rents for a given community. Class A office space varies by market.

most engineers in that he rarely trusted rules of thumb; he insisted on measuring everything and thinking through every design assignment like it was unique – which, as it turned out, was exactly the case. Every project in some way was unique.

After years of measuring buildings of all shapes and sizes around the United States, he understood how buildings "behaved" better than just about anyone in the business. When he and I took a close look at the proposed mechanical system of the new structure, we quickly learned that it was completely oversized. The local engineer's approach would waste a quarter of a million dollars of the client's money during construction above and beyond reasonable redundancy, and thousands annually in lost energy costs.

When we summarized our findings and presented them to the original engineer, he felt threatened and therefore simply dismissed them. The 1970s-era standards (at that point twenty years behind the times) he would use were fine, he insisted, and he refused to downsize the system to save the client money. In fact, he simply refused to believe that he could be wrong since he had "never had a complaint". He must have felt reluctant to admit his error on this one project after twenty years designing buildings in the same way, since it would likely mean having to admit many more errors from his past jobs.

So, based on his reaction we did what any rational person would do – we challenged him to back up his beliefs with measurement. "Prove it" we said.

What data did he have on his past designs that would show us how much energy this building would likely use? He had none. In twenty years, he had not measured any of his prior buildings to determine how efficiently they ran or how much energy was actually used. He was a principal in a major firm and yet not unique in this regard.

He was confident, he said, that his buildings were "state of the art." He received few complaints and we were simply wrong in his opinion. So we continued to push him – "How about we measure some of your recently constructed buildings that are similar so that we can compare the energy used in those to the energy that this new design will use? You can pick the buildings and have one of your engineers go with us and help measure," we said cheerily. "Fine," he said, and he even went so far as to say, "If you're right I'll gladly downsize the system and present the findings to the client." Ron and I were pleased.

A few weeks later Ron and I returned with one of his engineers to two of his buildings, similar in size and use to the one we were studying. Like the project we were consulting on, these buildings had grossly oversized systems. We knew it – they did not. We performed our analysis and found that these existing buildings were using approximately one fifth of the capacity during the prime cooling season that they were sized for. Their junior engineer, who was measuring with us, was amazed. We felt vindicated knowing that we had shown this engineer how to greatly improve efficiency while saving money upfront – immediate payback simply by making the system smaller.

Unfortunately, the story did not end on a positive note. After reviewing the data, the engineer of record went back on his word and refused to downsize his system at all. Worse, he preemptively went to the owner of the development (with whom he had a long relationship) and told him that we were making "irresponsible recommendations that were going to make him lose tenants by making people uncomfortable." He deliberately misled his client into wasting hundreds of thousands of dollars merely to save face. As outside consultants, we lost the battle since the client chose to believe the person he had known much longer.

The moral of this story: sometimes people care more about being right and fearing change than they do about finding the truth. Although Ron and I had too little sway to affect change in this specific project, our efforts showed the crucial role of measurement, and the importance of doing something with the resulting data. On many other projects, measurement has made the difference between success and failure.

SHEDDING LIGHT

Around this same time in my career, I purchased a light meter[3] for our company. It was the first time our office of nearly one hundred architects had ever had a piece of measuring equipment. Increasingly, we were using daylighting[4] strategies to reduce energy use in our buildings by offsetting the need for electric lighting and I felt the need to begin measuring some of our past work to see how effective we actually were.

For years, the industry standard for office buildings was to design lighting systems that provided "fifty footcandles"[5] of illumination at thirty inches above floor level (desk height). Lighting a space to this brightness level requires a significant amount of energy and, depending on the light source, a significant amount of heat to be generated within a space from the lights. There was nothing particularly magical or effective about the fifty footcandle standard since lighting effectiveness has more to do with a range of conditions in a space including how the light is delivered, the task being

---

[3] Light meters measure the amount of light allowed into a space, measured in terms of footcandles or lux.

[4] Daylighting is the practice of using natural light to illuminate the interior of a building while carefully controlling unwanted glare and heatgain.

[5] A footcandle is a unit of illumination based on the amount of light one candle gives off at a distance one foot from the point of measurement.

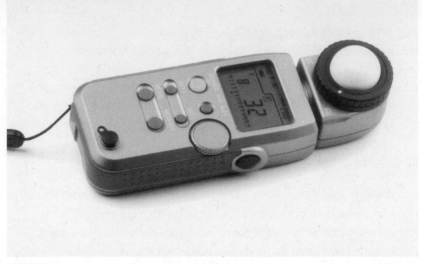

Light Meter

performed, the color of surfaces in the field of vision, the age of the
people in the space and a host of other factors that make any given
footcandle number an arbitrary value. As a dynamic organism, the
human eye constantly recalibrates based on the brightness of all
objects within its field of vision. It is all about context. As it turns
out, for most work-related tasks, fifty footcandles is excessive; for
some endeavors, it is insufficient. But the standard "stuck" for many
years[6], and most lighting specifications were based on it. Made
worse, mechanical engineers then sized their cooling systems based
on the heat load of fifty footcandle-based lighting systems and often
stuck with them even when lighting loads were considerably lower as
designed by their own electrical engineers!

A well-designed interior that avoids excessive glare from daylight and
has light-colored surfaces in the field of vision can be perfectly lit

[6] Thankfully, typical lighting levels have started to come down since the 1980s
and 1990s due to increased concern over energy use.

with only twenty-five to thirty footcandles, resulting in a nearly 50 percent reduction in energy savings and also reduced cooling loads.

So, for several months I began measuring every space I could with a light meter. I took it with me to offices we designed and buildings that others designed. I tracked data across various conditions – differing building types, ceiling heights, wall colors, and so on. I measured light levels with lights off at various times of the day under different sky conditions, then at various levels of dimming. It was fascinating. In most cases, our spaces were overlit and energy was being wasted. People would turn on lights simply because they were there, even when they had plenty of light for the work that they were doing.

I began to test myself before measuring to see if I could guess the footcandles based on the conditions. After a while, I became quite good at it – almost always outguessing lighting designers that I would work with since they too had not measured. Soon, I was able to walk into a space and approximate its footcandle level even before measuring it with the light meter. If one did not know better they would think I could actually visually tell the difference of light levels – but this was not the case. The human eye on its own can not tell the difference between twenty to thirty footcandles. It is actually impossible to walk into a space and "see" that a space has a given level of light. But it is possible for the human brain to learn patterns. I began to estimate light levels based on recurring design elements, lighting systems, colors and daylight conditions. With enough data, powerful observational correlations can be made.

Is this not a good metaphor for life?

My ability to gauge a room's necessary light had nothing to do with a physiological capability to discern the difference between thirty or fifty footcandles. It had nothing to do with "gut" intuition. It was about recognizing conditions and patterns only made visible through detailed and disciplined measurement. By taking the time to test our assumptions often and looking carefully at the trends that emerge we can surprise ourselves at what we can then, in fact, truly see.

REAL-WORLD EXAMPLES

The beauty of measuring is that it can be a very simple process. Here are three examples of how measurement led to awareness, which led to change:

What a Waste. A good friend and former colleague, Brad Nies, wanted to reduce the amount of refuse his household generated. He decided to track his patterns over a two-month period by sorting and weighing his trash and recycling every day. He recorded his findings in a journal. Very quickly, the data revealed patterns regarding the home's daily solid waste output. Simply becoming aware of his habits enabled Brad to change his purchasing decisions, which drastically reduced his trash load. The experiment was easy, and led to important change.

What a Charge. One of my favorite features of my electric car (the Sparrow) was a gauge on its dashboard that offered a real-time measurement of how much power remained on the battery. (Anytime you can get continuous, real-time monitoring, do it!) Driving an electric car means having to pay close and constant attention to this volt meter in order to avoid running out of "juice" while away from a plug-in power source. I monitored the meter vigorously, and began to understand explicitly the difference in how much energy a car utilizes while going uphill as opposed to downhill, how speed affects energy use and how driving styles can play a critical role in range. Right before my eyes, the gauge would register wasted energy if I accelerated too quickly given certain road conditions. This tool helped me change the way I drove, and gave me the data I needed to maximize the car's energy efficiency. There are people known as "hyper-milers" who use this knowledge to squeeze every drop of efficiency out of their vehicles. Some get twice the mpg that their cars are expected to achieve simply by paying attention (although with admittedly weird and sometimes annoying driving practices).

What a Catch. My friend, Niaz Dorry, is an activist who was named a Hero of the Planet by *Time Magazine* for her efforts to clean up the fisheries industry. Niaz has spent much of her career educating about the environmental, economic and local impacts of industrial fishing methods and their effects on local communities. By collecting data, tracking patterns, uncovering unhealthy practices and then communicating them, Niaz has helped reveal that large-scale fishing operations deplete resources and employ too few people relative to the size of the catch. As she says to many fishermen "you guys are trying to make a living while the factories are making a killing." Her straightforward wisdom (including the simple reminder to avoid buying fish that does not look like a fish, such as what you would find at a fast food restaurant selling fishburgers and fishsticks which almost certainly comes from industrial fishing) help American consumers support responsible fishing.

SWEATING THE BIG STUFF

If we get bogged down in the minutiae of our lives in our attempts to be green, we will drive ourselves crazy. The point of measuring everything for a period of time is not to then worry and stress about every single impact or behavior. It is to uncover the difference between the big stuff and the small stuff – which are sometimes surprising and often not what we first expected. Measuring shows us patterns in what we do so that we can change these patterns and the resulting effects.

Worrying about the environmental impact of every tiny detail becomes paralyzing and depressing. Instead, I believe we make much more of a difference when we pay attention to the big stuff. But often we do not have a good sense as to what truly is the "big stuff" vs the "small stuff". When we do what we can to understand our patterns regarding the amount of energy our homes consume, the cars we drive, the distances we travel, the products we purchase and the politicians we elect, we do the planet much more good.

It is not possible to be a saint, nor to have the impact of an ant. And the pursuit of perfection tends to alienate and demotivate since it is so difficult to achieve. But while we can not be perfect, we can improve almost any aspect of our lives through understanding. Whether it is the trash you generate or the mechanical system you design, measuring well can provide incredible insights and enlightenment and allow us to act with confidence.

It is impossible to create profound change without understanding what we hope to change. By measuring and observing, we gain awareness – the most critical first step on the path to change.

THE SUSTAINABLE DESIGN KNOWLEDGE ROSE

Years ago, I came across a simple graphing exercise in a European science journal (unrelated to building sciences). I was fascinated by the use of the circle to chart varying levels of information. I adapted the fundamental design to suit an idea of mine, and came up with the Sustainable Design Knowledge Rose.[7]

---

[7] The circle graph served as the basis of Bob Berkebile's, Noisette Rose, a tool for measuring community performance. I later used a similar design for the Pharos Material Evaluation tool shown in Chapter 15.

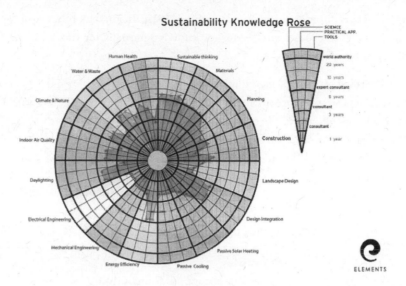

Sustainability Knowledge Rose

The knowledge rose is a self-evaluation tool I designed to help individuals expand their knowledge of sustainable design by identifying the strengths and weaknesses of their current knowledge base. The tool can be used to chart progress over time, to set goals or even to evaluate the distribution of sustainable design expertise within a team or office. Like many self-evaluation tools, the rose is only as useful as the individual is honest, meaning that people must self-assess with relative accuracy. The tendency is for individuals with less experience to overestimate their knowledge base, while those with more experience will tend to judge more accurately or even downplay their score. (The more you know, after all, the more you realize that you need to know.)

The tool operates by defining the major categories relevant to the sustainable design process. The actual number of categories and names of categories can be manipulated by individuals to describe knowledge for any discipline, such as interior design, landscape architecture, or mechanical engineering. In addition, the technique can be used to create "sub" roses, or knowledge roses for individual slices of the pie.

The exercise gives an individual a snapshot of where his or her strengths and weaknesses lie graphically. The rose is organized with multiple "pie slices" that represent fields of knowledge relevant to the overall field of green architecture or sustainable design. Most of these pies are further subdivided into three sections (with just a few exceptions). These three sections from left to right represent:

- Theoretical knowledge of the subject (pure science)
- Practical knowledge (hands-on)
- Tools of the trade

These distinctions are meant to recognize that individuals may have strong theoretical understanding of particular issues but little practical experience. It may also suggest that a person may have a clear understanding of the tools of the trade, but little understanding of why things work the way they do. Visualizing such differences in the three categories can help individuals work on improving or rounding out their knowledge base.

Each of these pie slices has a scale that runs from the center of the rose, describing no knowledge of the subject, to the outer edge representing world-class knowledge in that area. These concentric circles help to map performance as you move from topic to topic.

In a daylighting pie, for example, an individual may have a strong theoretical understanding of the behavior of light, how light reflects and how people see, but little understanding of how to design and construct a properly daylit space, and only a working knowledge of the tools to help predict light levels and the amount of contrast inherent.

Part of the importance of this tool is for individuals to learn two distinct lessons:

- It is impossible to become an expert in all aspects of sustainable design, which becomes apparent when someone accurately maps out their range of experience. One should not become discouraged however, as...

- It is desirable to create a solid, well-rounded base in order to understand all aspects of sustainability on a basic level and then develop special expertise in just a few categories. Many specialists lose perspective because of limited understanding of how their discipline relates to others.

In order to fill out the chart, one needs merely to begin to assess his or her skills in each topic area for each subcategory.

A few categories essential to sustainable design are not easily subdivided into theory and practical knowledge and are left as solid pies. These tend to be larger "catch all" categories that deserve their own knowledge roses. While it is more difficult to accurately assess a person's abilities in these categories, they tend to be so essential that they cannot be omitted. In many ways, what matters less is the overall score but the differences between categories or within pies that illustrate trends – the gaps in knowledge, so to speak. So even if someone grossly overestimates his or her knowledge base, the rose will at least judge relative expertise across categories.

This powerful graphing tool is easily adapted to many uses for people wanting to increase their effectiveness in their chosen career. New versions of the knowledge rose will be made available through time on the Zugunruhe website.

GWERSI XXI

Developing rules of thumb for things you do is fine,

As long as the rules do not become sacred.

Test assumptions often and be open to new possibilities when assumptions are wrong.

Formulate, test, reformulate, test.

Then repeat.

GWERSI XXII

When placed in a new situation or even a familiar one, do not assume that you know the answer.

Find a way to measure and learn directly what is happening.

Intuitive knowledge is strengthened through a deep understanding of reality.

Measure and analyze.

12

BECOMING A TRIM TAB:
BECOMING A LEVER FOR POWERFUL CHANGE

"Give me a lever long enough and a fulcrum on which
to place it, and I shall move the world."

—ARCHIMEDES

The Archimedes quote on the previous page is cited regularly and is often quoted frequently in business books. It is popular because it illustrates the power of leverage in order to make change. It is not enough simply to exert effort in order to make change; what matters most is how we go about making change. Nobody wants to work hard and achieve little. Identifying and utilizing the appropriate lever and fulcrum can turn effort into powerful results. Zugunruhe is a call to action – a compelling urge to seek change for the benefit of society, the environment and future generations. To be effective, however, requires that an individual learns the concept of leverage and can identify opportunities when time spent will result in a huge amplification of results.

ILLUSTRATING THE POINT

When I started as CEO of the Cascadia Green Building Council, one of my employees asked me what Cascadia was going to "be" under my direction. Instead of responding verbally, I took out a piece of paper and drew a simple illustration of a single piece of wood.

It looked like this:

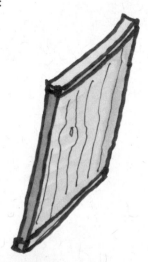

"What is it?" she asked, a bit perplexed.

"It's a trim tab" I replied, having fun with the vagueness of my answer and the befuddlement of my employee.

"All right, I'll bite," she said. "What's a trim tab?"

I returned to the paper and completed the drawing by adding a second piece of wood adjacent to the first and attaching both to a sketch of a boat.

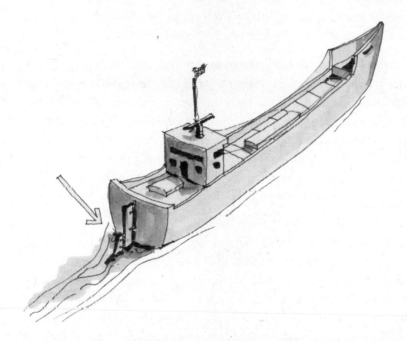

"You've drawn a rudder," she said, smiling. "I get it. We're going to help steer the green movement."

"Yes," I agreed. "But this metaphor means much more than that."

I went on to explain myself and my drawing. A trim tab, I told her, is a tiny rudder placed below a larger rudder on substantial ocean-going vessels. Relative to its counterpart, the trim tab is insignificant in size. But without it, the main rudder would be useless and the ship would be unable to turn as the rudder alone was simply not powerful enough to do its job. It is, in effect, a lever acting on a lever – a very tiny device that has huge power and influence. An intriguing example of the very principle to which Archimedes referred. But there is more to this story. In order to compel the rudder to turn the boat, the trim tab actually moves in the opposite direction of the rudder. To create change, it goes down a completely divergent path. Isn't that interesting?

To my mind, the trim tab is the most fantastic real-world example of how individuals and organizations can make change that is seemingly disproportionate to their own size and scale, and accomplish change by steering away from the mainstream. It shows that it is possible to be a lever acting upon another lever harnessing the efforts of much larger entities, so that even the smallest of us can create profound change. Buckminster Fuller was a huge proponent of the trim-tab metaphor and it guided his thinking a great deal. Bucky understood leverage.

While not everyone has the individual influence or resources to be a "rudder," anyone can become a trim tab. We can look at initiatives, ideas and whole organizations that are struggling to make change and seek ways to intervene, amplify and improve upon their success. All around us are opportunities where small efforts can provide great results. Doing so only requires that we begin to see the world as full of such opportunities for leverage.

THE APPLE AND THE TREE

Apple® is one of the finest examples of a corporation that thinks like a trim tab even though it has now become large enough to be a full-fledged rudder in several market segments. Apple recognizes the risks associated with developing new technology, so it rarely invents its own products. Instead, it takes a trim tab attitude by adapting competitive innovations to suit the preferences of the target audiences it knows so well using design and visionary thinking. Apple looks for the highest point of leverage, repackages products and transforms user experiences in new and different ways.

The iPod is the most obvious example. Mp3 players had been on the market for several years before Apple repurposed the technology, put a sexy new spin on the idea, tied the concept to a music purchasing site and kicked off a global marketing phenomenon. The iPod became a trim tab for change that has overhauled the way music is bought, sold and experienced throughout the world. Apple now controls more than 70 percent of the global digital music player market as a result of understanding the power of leverage.

Apple applied the same approach when it launched the iPhone, repackaging existing technologies and ideas and revolutionizing telecommunications. In its first year on the market, the iPhone earned *Time Magazine's* top invention of the year honors. There are now hundreds of thousands of "apps" sold on the itunes store – a brilliant move that leverages the innovations of thousands of companies to make the iphone more desireable. It is quickly becoming the most sought after phone in the world.[1]

A GREEN TRIM TAB

In the green building world, the U.S. Green Building Council (USGBC) is a powerful example of the trim tab concept. Established in 1996 as a unifying organization for the various factions dedicated to green

---

[1] Time will tell if the iPad has the same impact.

building, the USGBC is now one of the largest and most influential non-profits in America with the ability to steer the entire industry. In effect, the USGBC began as a trim tab and quickly emerged as the movement's rudder.

What is particularly interesting about the USGBC story is that the organization was founded simply as a mechanism to bring together the multiple specialties within the green building community, and assist them in focusing their efforts. The USGBC belonged to no one group – it was neither heavily represented nor influenced by architects, engineers, designers, contractors or government agencies. Instead, it existed to benefit all those who participated in the green movement. Each discipline did good work, but worked as a silo without a unifying set of guidelines. USGBC served as the trim tab to the industry's rudder, uniting the specialties under one banner. But the industry was so ready for direction that the USGBC, along with the LEED standards it developed, quickly became the rudder itself. As Paul Hawken has publicly declared, the USGBC does more to further the green building movement and enable real change than dozens of non-governmental organizations (NGOs) combined.

Just as the USGBC led to the development of LEED standards, LEED standards opened the door to the possibility of the Living Building Challenge (detailed in Chapter 9). Now that green building practices are more widely accepted and LEED standards are more commonly met, the Living Building Challenge (LBC) ups the ante by asking even more of the building community. In this sense, the LBC is the trim tab on the USGBC rudder. By leveraging the recently elevated interest in green building, LBC takes it one step further and defines a greater goal – the endgame strategy for the built environment. In 1997, when LEED standards were first introduced, people felt that the platinum level was the farthest (and greenest) point to which sustainable building could be taken. LBC seeks to extend that end point, since the industry has proven it can meet the platinum goals on building projects all over the continent.

LOOKING WITHIN

"A soul without a high aim is like a ship without a rudder."
—Eileen Caddy

Acting like a trim tab requires time to think and reflect, since intrinsically it has to be strategic and not merely reactive. One must be a polymath with good mentorship and a keen understanding of how to make effective change to be a trim tab. And the goal must always be to initiate profound change. It helps to look first to our own lives, asking what we can control, how can we leverage change within ourselves, and how we can move beyond the spheres of influence that surround us. Most importantly, we must commit to doing more than good work...we must do good work effectively.

Being a "trim tab for change" requires:

- Pursuing strategic collaboration with multiple "rudders" and other trim-tab groups instead of seeing competition and "winning" as the goal.

- Complementing rather than duplicating the work of others – helping to make something existing better or finding places where a new intervention can elevate an overall effort.

- Investing a level of effort that is comparable to the amount of desired change – being willing to work extremely hard but without burning yourself out.

- Resisting the urge to act too foolishly and arrogantly act as a rudder ourselves by tackling issues that are beyond our own resources and knowledge – a sure path to ineffectiveness and frustration.

- Becoming comfortable with the idea of potentially countering popular sentiment or the way things are usually done– change is not always popular and conflict can be counted on.

ACTING ON OPPORTUNITIES

"Change starts when someone sees the next step."
—William Drayton

During my years at BNIM, I was surrounded by talented people who did important and beneficial work. We devoted ourselves personally and professionally to change in every project we were involved with. Yet sometimes, despite our best efforts, projects failed. I participated in a number of significant projects that had great potential but never ended up getting built. I often felt frustrated after working diligently for several years on a given job, only to have the project disappear for some reason or another – economic, political, etcetera. When these projects went away so too did valuable work, ideas and designs. It always seemed to me that this kind of knowledge and experience earned deserved to exist farther out in the public realm, owned by more than just a single client with lots of resources.

So in 1999, I founded Elements, the green consulting division of the firm and one of the first of its kind on the continent[2]. The philosophy was simple: provide sustainable consulting services to competitive design firms (and internally within BNIM) in order to broaden the industry-wide understanding of green building practices and push the knowledge outward (while making profit for our company).

---

[2] In recent years, green teams have sprouted up in almost every major firm. Elements was the first of its kind.

At first, many thought we were crazy to assist our competitors. Surely we were giving up our "trade secrets" and relinquishing our competitive advantage! But we knew better. We understood that helping the larger goal of greening the industry was more important than protecting our professional egos. We also understood that by consulting to others, we were simultaneously making several smart business moves for our own organization:

- We were solidifying our reputation as the true "experts" in the marketplace.

- We were learning new ways to communicate the information we knew – building the overall market helped us more than our competitors.

- We were reaching into new markets and getting exposed to significantly more project types and clients helping to diversify our experience.

- We were always learning what others in our industry knew and what they did not know so we could stay one step ahead.

The experiment ended up being a success, and served as an important trim tab for numerous projects all over the country, while helping to grow our business internally.

From there, I looked for additional ways to leverage my knowledge and connections to enable further change. Having seen the impact Paul Hawken's books made, I founded Ecotone Publishing (www. ecotonedesign.com) to ensure that information about green building was readily available to those who sought it. The lever lengthened and the fulcrum strengthened, and I published my first book, which has now been used in more than more than seventy universities and colleges across the continent and is available for purchase globally[3]. Through Ecotone, I published the works of other experts and extended the reach and quality of the green building message.

My decision to join Cascadia was rooted in my belief that I need to do all I can to continue the momentum of these message-spreading exercises. As the reality of climate change and other globally significant environmental challenges has become more apparent, organizations such as Cascadia present the opportunity to help hundreds of firms from all backgrounds in their green efforts. But the leaders of these organizations must be willing to let go of a certain amount of ego and personal gratification, and allow the success of others to take the spotlight. Just as an architect creates tangible works that incorporate and display his or her design talents, an educator enables others to grow and shine and he or she must be satisfied with that background role. Much like a trim tab. In any endeavor there are ways to harness your experience by finding new business opportunities – new markets, new services that can help you amplify your effectiveness.

STEERING ONESELF TOWARD CHANGE

"The entrepreneur always searches for change, responds to it, and exploits it as an opportunity."
—Peter F. Drucker

Once we have decided to take action – to be moved by our passion and our beliefs – we must ask ourselves "what next?" What kinds of actions do we take? How can we get the most strategic impact from what we do? Even leaders of corporate and government entities

---

[3] It was recently translated into Korean as well.

must ask themselves these same questions if they want to work toward change.

As you seek ways in which you can serve as a trim tab, look for:

- Groups or individuals doing good work but lacking in some key resource that you could provide
- Work that nobody is doing yet that would add value to a greater effort
- Work that is being done on an old paradigm that could be reinvented or recreated
- Work that needs a new "story" or medium or presentation
- Work that is already being done but for which you could help supply a new audience
- Work that is being pushed in the wrong direction that you could help steer toward a more effective solution or model
- Work that is being done well in another region or venue that you could bring closer to home

Basically, we must ask ourselves how to create new fulcrums for levers that are already in place. Creating profound change is not always about reinventing the wheel. Sometimes it is about discovering new forms of leverage.

G W E R S I   X X I I I

When ready to act,

First look to understand how your actions, skills and contributions can do the most good.

Harness the works of others.

Look for ways to leverage change,

And for opportunities for interventions that bring cascading effects.

GWERSI XXIV

Regardless of where you are in your career,

There are always opportunities to make change.

Look for them

And try to find places to intervene where you can
leverage your skills and knowledge.

Do not hesitate.

Begin.

13

SLAVES TO PROCESS:
CHANGE THE SYSTEM TO CHANGE THE RESULT

"I am a man of fixed and unbending principles, the first of which is to be flexible at all times."

—EVERETT DIRKSEN

"Stay committed to your decisions, but stay flexible in your approach."

—TOM ROBBINS

Continuously reinventing the wheel is inefficient. To make progress, we develop systems, procedures and rules of thumb on which we can rely again and again. Yet even a system that at one point increased efficiency and success can, at another time, hinder accomplishments and efficiency. It is difficult to get much done in most lines of work without some type of system or procedures in place, but paradoxically, the very machinery that helps move things forward often can cripple true progress, revolutionary developments and profound change.

I have seen a lot of good ideas get bogged down in bureaucratic processes, and a lot of talented people get sidetracked within the systems they set up to help them make informed decisions. What starts out as efficiency improvements begin to take on a life of their own to the point where further progress and personal or professional growth is stymied. This sequence is typical of any great movement, business or organization. In the start-up stages, things are chaotic and fast moving and participants remain flexible because they believe they have no choice. Then structures begin to fall into place that support the growth of the organization or cause and help to weed out inefficiencies – a maturing occurs. In many cases, these structures transform as they become institutionalized. Ultimately, processes, procedures, rules and systems can begin to dominate the mission and catastrophic imbalance sets in. The result — an inevitable decline. Conversely, the movements and entities that endure recognize that all systems need to change as new realities emerge.

Nature provides us with wonderful examples of how not to get stuck in habitual patterns of behavior, as change is necessary for survival. As a tree grows, it adjusts constantly to respond to external forces. Each year brings a slightly different level of growth to different parts of the tree as rainfall, available sunlight and other climate conditions vary annually. Boughs reach in new directions depending on the amount of available light and the proximity of nearby trees, also adjusting on a constant basis. In essence, the tree redefines its process and structure continuously at every moment because of ever-changing inputs. If only human-made systems were so elegant. Our systems are reactions to a reality that is merely a snapshot in time – then rarely revisited. Once we create a system our tendency is to fall in love with it!

GREEN BABY STEPS

"When you only have a hammer, everything looks like a nail."
—Anonymous

When we aim for big change, process is enormously important. Without some sort of operating rules, nothing organized and effective will happen and change will seldom occur. But when there is a disproportionate amount of focus on process, it is easier for us to lose track of our goals. We all know people who describe themselves as "process oriented". Watch out for them – and resist the urge to emulate too closely how they operate. Process people are rarely the harbingers of profound change. The main reason is that they begin to associate their own identity "I'm process oriented" with the procedures they put in place. Straying from "their process" feels to them like straying from who they are. If you are a process-oriented person – take a long hard look at your assumptions and the level of attachment you have to "your way of doing things" as your path to Zugunruhe may actually be stymied before you even begin.

The environmental movement is at a critical point in its development. I believe that in order for it to truly succeed, it needs to fundamentally change itself. The old way of promoting environmental issues through campaigns of guilt and shame have proven only marginally successful. And yet many organizations stay rooted in their same paradigms even as their memberships fall and their effectiveness diminishes. Just as the planet is in constant flux, so too should our ideas and the approaches to realize them. We are not fighting the same battle a decade onwards – rarely are our challenges truly the same even from year to year.

Let's use a building example again. The realities of construction dictate that we adhere to certain systems and protocols. Building codes, for example, force a degree of process rigor upon designers and engineers. Architects, engineers and contractors repeat specific processes and pursue solutions that have worked in the past – simply because they did not fail or did not raise a red flag relative to certain codes. These past design solutions often hamstring future solutions because they become imbedded in our "given assumptions" and are not revisited even after new technologies or techniques have the potential to change the outcome – so the realm of possible solutions becomes a smaller box.

But I think we typically have much more freedom than we allow ourselves, and we self-limit more than necessary because we are accustomed to certain invisible boundaries that lie between us, our colleagues and our aspirations. We do things certain ways because the last time we tried it, it did not fail or because it is comfortable, safe, familiar. Sometimes, we do things in certain ways for no better reason than habit or worse as I already described because we begin to identify that particular solution with "how I do it". The solution becomes a signature – part of our identity – and then it blinds us. We begin to look for anything that justifies how our process is correct and ignore signs that it is not.

Long-time green building professionals and environmentalists spent years in a paradigm of being marginalized, constantly having to fight uphill battles for even the smallest conservation gains. People developed strategies to deal with the frustration that arose from constant battles lost, which typically included the soul-killing paradigm of "settling" and mission drift. Tacit acceptance born from battle weary cynicism that produced rationalizations became the norm, such that any incremental improvement was seen as success even when it should not have been.

For thirty years, green warriors had to be accustomed to the glacial speed with which mainstream society historically heard our message. Because of this tradition, the movement has grown in "baby steps" – tiny, incremental forward motion is the rule rather than the exception. However, the recent spike in climate change awareness has shed new light on and created new interest in the movement. Rising energy prices, international uncertainty and the struggling economy is making our message more relevant, useful and powerful than ever before at the same time that the stakes could not be higher. Based on the predictions of all the world's leading climate scientists, we have a scant amount of time[1] to make transformative changes to the way we use energy and the amount of carbon our activities release. Somehow, our movement must shed the weight of the paradigm of the last thirty years and take bolder action if we are to succeed. With only a few seconds left on the clock it is time for major pass plays, not a running game, to use a football analogy. Our baby steps must now turn into giant leaps, and our processes must accommodate this new pace and the urgency behind it.

OLD DOGS, OLD TRICKS, OLD RESULTS

In previous chapters, we have touched on how attitude, more than technological or economic factors, is one of the primary barriers to

---

[1] According to the Intergovernmental Panel on Climate Change (IPCC) we have less than a decade to make significant changes to our economies to drastically reduce carbon emissions.

a truly sustainable future. Even when groups of people have the best intentions, self-limiting factors emerge in how they attempt to mobilize, make change or sway decisions. Old habits die hard, after all. Unfortunately for all of us, these very patterns of behavior that we have difficulty shaking are what cause most of the problems.

The bottom line here is that when we want a different result, we must approach the problem differently than we have in the past. Obvious, perhaps, but difficult to apply to real-world challenges. Architect William McDonough has said, "Design is the first signal of human intention." I would add that it is the systems we put in place that allow our intentions to succeed or fail. Reflection, I believe, is the signal for effective change.

To be successful, we must check all assumptions at the door and re-evaluate the way we do things. How do we make decisions as individuals? How does our group do so? What rules are already in place? Do those rules work, given the goals at hand? Is the effort effective? What new information should be used to inform our thinking and our systems?

EXAMPLES FROM THE FIELD:

- I have seen architects who are wholeheartedly interested in transforming the environmental impacts of their building designs, yet do so without stopping to change their approach to design. They assume somehow that their intention is enough; merely "willing" a green project to happen or simply tacking on green features at the end of the design process will end in the right results. Not surprisingly, the results are always less than stellar, and these designers can not understand why they were not successful. Worse yet, they begin to believe that their goals were never achievable.

If you want a different outcome, changing how you do something is mandatory.

- I have seen design professionals whose clients push them toward green design, but they resist because the approach requires a new way of thinking, new materials and new systems. Their disbelief in the potential success of any new reality leads them to hedge their bets, and they end up with an even more conservative, less green end-product than they could have easily achieved. People often feel threatened on some level by new approaches, as to them it feels like their "old ways of doing things" are now shown to be wrong.

- I have seen green building or environmental groups begin collaborations, driven by a sense of great urgency, only to spend months discussing and arguing about how they should make decisions, what they believe in and how they should communicate their beliefs. In the end, they achieve very little and act without the urgency they themselves espouse. Spend most of your time on actual work – and only as much time on process as absolutely necessary, knowing it will change as conditions change. This realization should make process itself less sacred.

- I have seen groups that are driven more by a desire to build consensus and "keep everyone happy" than to accomplish the goals at hand. Such "designs by committee" usually result in mediocre solutions, even when highly talented people are involved. Working independently, these same participants could have produced more valuable results in half the time – working together with effective leadership –even more.

TAKING PROCESS WITH A GRAIN OF SALT

Process is no more than a tool. When it does not help get the job done, it must be set aside and replaced with a more effective implement. For some reason, though, we struggle with changing our protocols that feel fundamental to the way we do things. Pride, fear and laziness all stand in the way, even when we know something must change.

When we get past the point of simply wanting change, and we are ready to create it, here are some ways to stir the process pot:

Do not take any process or procedure too seriously. There is no intrinsic value in process except for the result to which it leads. The amount of time that goes into figuring out a process is irrelevant if that process is no longer working. If you find yourself justifying a system simply because it took a great deal of time to create, and you feel you must honor the work invested in designing it, that is a red flag. If the system is not working, fix it.

Let go of ego. Group dynamics sometimes dictate that the stronger, louder voices are the only ones heard, and those occupying the ladder's "lower rungs" are less worthy of attention. But flawed systems are often legacies of old leaders. So be sure to listen to the input of all players, remembering that the best idea, whatever its origin, benefits the entire group and furthers the cause. The point is not that everyone has an equal vote (watch out for consensus decisions) but that everyone's ideas receive equal consideration. The best idea wins.

Do not associate yourself with the process. Sometimes, people fall in love with the processes they use to the extent that they even identify personally with them. "This is just how I do it" or "Our group has always done it this way" can be dangerous excuses, particularly when they lead to poor results. The process should lead to the goal, not limit its success.   Successful individuals disassociate themselves with their processes and procedures and remain nimble.

Keep the lid to the toolkit open. If you need a hammer and all you have is a screwdriver, you do not keep trying to screw in the nail. If a process worked perfectly the last time, by all means, use it again. But if it worked in a less-than-ideal fashion, then abandon it and create a new way that takes you closer to your desired outcome. For profound change to occur, we must realize that there are exceptions to all systems, protocols and rules.

THE PROS AND CONS OF DYNAMIC GOVERNANCE: A CASE STUDY

In green design (in particular, the world of the U.S. Green Building Council and its large chapter network), there is a strong trend toward a process known as dynamic governance.[2] Dynamic governance is used to make group decisions in many green building organizations. As a tool, dynamic governance can be very useful to move a contentious issue to resolution, especially to unite disparate groups and build consensus.

For the uninitiated, here is how it works: Dynamic governance is a decision-making protocol that allows discussion and proposals to happen until a solution is proposed to which nobody has a paramount objection. If there is a paramount objection by anyone – even a single individual in a large group – then, in theory, the group continues the dialogue until a palatable resolution can be achieved. The underlying philosophy is inclusiveness and a desire to bring everyone to a point of consensus and decision. It is a politically correct way to create solutions, and in certain instances can be highly effective. It is

---

[2] Dynamic Governance is a form of Sociocracy – a form of governance using consent-based decision-making.

usually presented with the best intentions, and it is unquestionably set up to treat everyone fairly, which in some situations is a huge leap forward over strictly command and control decision making.

The problem is that once it has been used successfully, many groups then abuse it and try to use it for all of their decision making, often for negative long-term impact. Constantly and religiously sticking to a process where everyone has an equal voice and a single individual can hold up group decisions places too much importance on not offending and not enough importance on seeking the highest and best solution. The process can easily begin to highjack the result.

The hard truth, whether politically correct or not, is that not everyone's opinion is of equal wisdom and depth in all situations. Giving everyone's ideas equal consideration is not the same thing as giving everyone an equal vote. Consensus can produce mediocre results when more powerful options are actually available. Even more problematic is when the vested interests of a few hold back progress of a whole group. Sometimes, in our efforts to treat all players fairly, we dishonor the levels of contributions people make, their experience and talents. In this way, I have seen dynamic governance have a tendency to prevent truly innovative ideas from taking shape, since they often come with risk and are then bound to generate paramount objections within group settings.

The truth is that dynamic governance, like integrated design, works in many settings – just not every setting. As a movement, we must recognize that systems and processes must cater to the challenge at hand, and adjust to meet the challenge. There is no perfect system. A single organization might use multiple decision-making protocols over the course of one meeting if necessary and beneficial – as long as the process itself does not begin to take too long. Deciding how you are going to decide, for example, should be done quickly and is the bane of so many meetings! Once again, it is useful to visualize the end goal first, then back-cast from that ideal scenario in order to design the most suitable process. Create a system, test it, and re-create if necessary.

WU WEI AND WATERY PERFECTION

"Nothing is softer or more flexible than water, yet nothing can resist it."
— Lao Tzu

When people get stuck in a rut or refuse to change their approach to problem solving, I often think of the Taoist concept of Wu Wei. Wu Wei has multiple interpretations, most of which deal with the notion of "effortless action," but it is universally associated with flexibility and openness to change. As such, it is the perfect philosophy to adopt when thinking about process.

Water, with its yielding nature, is the traditional symbol of Wu Wei. Paradoxically, water is soft and fluid enough to flow at will, yet hard enough to overpower even the most substantial stones and metals given time. It is formless, never forcing its own shape upon other substances and always traveling along the most efficient path. As conditions change, it has the ability to adjust its physical structure from liquid to gas or solid. Always in balance, water forever finds its own level state.

What a beautiful way to look at process. When we attempt to fit problems into certain systematic shapes that do not accommodate them, we may as well try to keep water from rolling off a stone. Once we learn to re-shape our processes to suit the problems we face, they will prove to be watertight.

G W E R S I   X X V

Spending too much time pondering how
something should be accomplished

Can be as destructive as spending too little.

The systems we use are not the result.

Therefore, spend the majority of your energy
on the actual effort

Rather than the approach to the effort.

GWERSI XXVI

If a given approach is not working, then change it.

If it is only working somewhat, then tweak it.

If it works as intended, then stick with it – with both eyes open.

Become separate from "how" you do things and you may become better acquainted with what you are doing and why.

14

THE NEW COLLABORATION:
THE GATHERING OF THE TRIBES

"When people ask me if we are simply preaching to the choir,
I like to remind them that the choir needs a lot of practice."
—DAVID KORTEN

When we step back and look at the daunting challenges we face as a society, as a movement and even as a species, it is easy to become disheartened. It is hard to visualize a better world when we stand within our current reality, amid a disturbing economic crisis and near-complete environmental apathy, even with uncontestable proof of dangerous climate change ahead. The change we seek seems out of reach, and yet, as change agents, we must resist the urge to buckle under such odds and become cynical and disinterested. It is extremely difficult to simultaneously embrace the reality that things are most likely going to get a whole lot worse for the majority of humanity and creation before it can possibly get better and yet remain positive and effective. It is hard to accept that reality and to soldier on regardless – optimistic, inspired, insightful and mostly unflappable[1]. Impossible, in fact, if we had to do it alone. Possible, only if we join the great migration that is underway and find those other individuals who, like you and I, are ready for profound internal and external change to occur.

I had an interesting experience recently while attending GreenBuild, the largest tradeshow and conference devoted to the green building industry in the world. Greenbuild is an amazing event, instrumental in helping many people get "religion" about green and introducing them to a world of new products and services. At least the first couple of times individuals atend they typically leave transformed, as the individuals suddenly find themselves not in a minority –but as part of a large turbulent flow of progressive energy. Those only partially excited about sustainability usually find something that compels them to open their eyes to a new way of thinking. It is a great place to start Zugunruhe typically. Over the years it has been the place to be for the most exciting new ideas launched to move the industry forward.

---

[1] I say "mostly" because everyone deserves to indulge in moments of hopelessness as long as one does not dwell there!

Yet, as I observed this particular Greenbuild and watched the flow of nearly thirty thousand people all focused on green building, the energy I sensed was not one of great migration. Somehow, perhaps due to the economy, the energy was disjointed and the sense of urgency I had come to expect was absent. Most participants were operating under the same paradigms that had gotten us into our current mess. As the show progressed, I found myself getting more and more depressed, as it was clear that despite the huge growth in general awareness, so few were ready for fundamental change. The level of dialogue required for truly transformative change was absent. At first it made me feel very alone; I wandered the halls of the convention center and I despaired at how little I felt we were all collectively doing to actually turn the ship around.

As the show ended and my mood worsened, I joined the final plenary speech to listen to E.O. Wilson and Janine Benyus have an intimate chat about the environment in front of about ten thousand people. It was amazing to watch these two wonderful intellects talk about nature and what it has to teach us. As their time winded down, they asked for questions and I felt compelled to stand up. I had to shake my despair and reconnect. There were microphones placed in the four corners of the hall and as I walked to the nearest one in this colossal exhibit hall, each microphone soon had a giant queue of people waiting to ask their question. I got in line to ask my question and waited.

The session was being broadcast live through the U.S. Green Building Council's website, and people all over the world were watching and listening. As often happens when I get a strong intuitive urge to act, a magical thing happened. My timing turned out to be uncanny, as I got to ask the last question and close out the show – which, given the numbers present, was really a slim chance. Originally intending to ask a question about the Living Building Challenge in order to get my program some valuable air time, I changed it on the spot and asked the question most pressing on my mind. "Hi, Janine," I said. Then, "Hello Mr. Wilson," (E.O Wilson is a huge hero of mine). "On behalf of everyone here, I want to thank both of you for what you have done to teach us," I began and the audience joined in with a thunderous applause of their appreciation for the two of them. As the applause died down, I said, "Given everything we are learning about how little time we have to make widespread change, how do we inspire each other to move faster and further and at a quicker pace?"

There was a pause… then Janine spoke up and said, "Jason, one of the things I would say is to remember that you are not alone." It was not the answer I was expecting, but it spoke to the heart of what I was feeling personally. I looked around. Thousands of expectant people on the edge of their seat anticipating the next words of the interchange – and suddenly all of us in the room were back in the same space – together. She then went on to talk about how, in any industry – chemistry, biology, manufacturing, agriculture, green building – in every sector of humanity there are people gathering and working and struggling with the same underlying questions. At times it feels very lonely and isolating – but in truth it is not. All over the world at this very instant there are thousands of people thinking and scheming around the same set of challenges. None of them are truly alone.

"And how do we speed up the rate of adaptation," she asked rhetorically before adding, "Nature uses co-evolutionary loops."

At the close she mentioned the flower and the hummingbird where my own story in this book began, and explained the idea that these two species increase their rate of adaptation by being in a relationship with each other. Together. They changed together, not alone. The more they cooperated, the greater the adaptation and resilience. Just like the wolf makes the deer faster and the deer in turn makes the wolf faster and more stealthful, it was through a co-evolutionary collaboration that significant change occurred. The inner migration so necessary to begin zugunruhe relies strongly on the outward migration – in a co-evolutionary process. We become more effective internally by reaching out externally and vice versa.

Our job, according to Benyus, is to "hook up with people re-imagining our world" in order to find others in their own zugunruhe. Together, the rate of adoption and adaptation will increase, as only together can a punctuated equilibrium[2] emerge.

I smiled as I sat down and suddenly...I felt much better. I spoke publicly about my concerns, and people responded and Janine, as she often does, hit the essence of what I was questioning. As I sat there though, an even more amazing thing happened. My cell phone started buzzing...several text messages streamed through from friends listening around the country both in the auditorium and a few who could not attend. People who in real time had heard my question – some from several thousand miles away listening to the broadcast – and then instantly sent me messages that they had heard me on the live streaming broadcast and really appreciated my question. The universe was responding in the form of texts and tweets! And as the show finished, another couple of dozen folks rushed forth to talk to me, excited and appreciative that I had asked the question that they too had on their minds.

Zugunruhe.

We are not alone.

---

[2] The evolutionary process involving long periods without change (stasis) punctuated by short periods of rapid speciation.

CREATING FUNDAMENTAL SOCIETAL CHANGE

I believe that it is possible to completely change the course of
our civilization within the span of a single life – changing from a
society built upon fossil fuels and corporatism to one based on true
community and sustainability – existing comfortably within a supply
of current solar income.[3]

Some might say it would be impossible to initiate such radical shifts
in the way our society exists. Surely political and corporate resistance
would overpower the efforts of those leading the environmental
charge? The problem with this line of thinking, though, is that it is
fraught with amnesia even if it often seems true. People forget that
if conditions are ripe for change due to hard times, war, political
and economic unrest, and/or the broad availability of new keystone
technologies, change can happen quite quickly and sometimes in
surprising or violent ways. Few could have predicted the fall of
the Berlin Wall and the complete societal restructuring in several
European countries a year or two earlier. There are also examples
of peaceful transitions that resulted in new, more positive societal
models. The history of the last couple of hundred years alone provides
many powerful examples of fundamental and revolutionary change.

ENSLAVED BY TRADITION

It was not very long ago that people of color were part of an economic
model of subjugation and slavery. The United States was built on
the backs of African Americans and other ethnic groups who had

---

[3] Current Solar Income is the idea of living off "interest" rather than depleting
"capital" when it comes to energy use. Relying on coal or petroleum or any non-
renewable fuel creates pollution and releases stored carbon. Solar and wind
and tidal power (the latter two are simply another form of solar energy) is using
energy "currently" available.

no rights and no freedoms. There were plenty of intelligent and well-educated individuals in the 19th-century who felt strongly that abolishing slavery would destroy the American economy and reduce their rights as "white Americans." They fought to hang onto this barbaric practice as their opponents fought to change the paradigm. While the country dealt with numerous challenges following the Civil War and many citizens were forced to accommodate the new realities of a free society, the national economy survived and thrived. The country become more influential, wealthy and powerful after slavery was abolished than before it.[4]

A JOINING OF FORCES DURING WW2

World War II historians often describe the powerful national economic integration and alignment that took place in the United States between the attack on Pearl Harbor in 1941 and the end of the war in 1945.[5] In the span of those four years, Americans banded together as part of "the war effort," amassing resources, community will and expertise. A great sharing of resources and ingenuity led to unprecedented growth and innovation. The literal and immediate nature of the threat at that time helps explain the willingness of so many citizens to sacrifice on behalf of the greater good. This nationalized endeavor opened the door to innovation and entrepreneurship that positioned the United States as a global

---

[4] Over a hundred years later there is still progress to be made, and yet it is true that in just a few years following the end of the Civil War the whole economy of the South was remade.

[5] Canadians entered the war in 1939 as soon as Britain joined and the Canadian war effort was instrumental in helping the Allied forces before the United States joined and tipped the scale. Like in the United States, the Canadian economy emerged from the ashes of the war as one of the top economies (and militaries) in the world.

economic leader, and ushered in an unprecedented era of prosperity. In many ways, the United States has coasted for the last several decades on the innovations introduced during these few years.

THE BUILT ENVIRONMENT IN POST-WW2 AMERICA

It may sound far-fetched to propose that America completely transform all of its built environment – homes, buildings, transportation and manufacturing facilities – within the next two to three decades in order to avoid the worst of climate change impacts. But people should not forget that a transition of that scale happened just a few decades earlier. Following World War II, great changes swept the United States and Canada. From the early 1950s through the late 1970s, virtually every city in North America rebuilt itself to adjust to the automobile-centric society rather than one that flows according to the comings and goings of human beings by slower methods of transportation. Cities for cars rather than cities for people and horses. Think about it. Since 1956, the American interstate system has grown so quickly that it could now extend from end to end and circumnavigate the globe twice. It is the largest public works project in history. Rural economies that previously supported more than half of America's population have rapidly given way to urban centers; the freeways offer workers a way to get there.[6] The point is that few people in 1945 could have envisioned such a wholesale transformation of the American landscape. Compare photos of any North American city in 1945 with that city in 1975/85 and you will be surprised at the scale of the transformation. Essentially every city, town, hamlet, suburb and village was completely changed. Surely we can change it again.

---

[6] Our interstates were originally designed for rapid military mobilization however.

LOOKING FORWARD

In my line of work, I encounter skepticism on a regular basis. Frequently, I speak with people who doubt that our society would ever be able to wean itself off the fuel-burning automobile and return to a way of designing cities around citizens rather than vehicles. If we look at current trends (the price of oil, and our tenuous financial systems, for example), it becomes obvious that we do not have much choice. Without a stable climate, continual economic growth, relative peace and affordable oil, the entire system on which we have built our cities changes dramatically. And what emerges on the other side could be much worse if we do not initiate changes immediately.[7] I predict that in the next thirty years and maybe yet this decade, our society will undergo a change that is fast and unpredictable. We will likely see the end of the oil era within our children's lifetime, and the end of globalism as we know it. In an era of peak oil, shipping products all over the planet will become a thing of the past. The flat world described by Friedman will begin to curve again. Ideas can be transported thousands of miles through our communications, but manufacturing goods will begin to occur in tighter concentric rings over the next couple of decades. Our cities will become less suburban and more urban, and food production and energy generation will begin to become more decentralized, local and sustainable. There will even be a rural resurgence – with true agricultural towns reemerging. As these changes occur, it will be our responsibility to watch over them carefully, helping to ensure the smoothest transition possible – not by working alone, but by working together in a new form of collaboration.

---

[7] I encourage people to read James Howard Kunstler's two recent books, *The Long Emergency* and the companion novel *World Made By Hand*.

THE GATHERING OF THE TRIBES

"We may have all come in different ships, but we are all in the same boat now."
—Martin Luther King, Jr.

"If you want to go fast, go alone. If you want to go far, go together."
—African Proverb

Since I was quite young, I have been fascinated with the history, culture and landscape of my Scottish ancestors.[8] My grandmother spoke a wee bit of Gaelic, and I had great interest in trying to understand how my family ended up in North America with so many others during the incredibly sad time known as the Highland Clearances. During the 18th and 19th centuries the famous Scottish clans were dismantled and families were uprooted and sometimes forcibly removed from their land. Thousands left Scotland to relocate in Canada, Australia, New Zealand and the United States. This exodus followed an earlier brutal period of several hundred years when my ancestors, the Scottish Celts, fought the English for sovereignty. Some of these struggles have been immortalized in film by the likes of Mel Gibson (playing William Wallace in "Braveheart") and Liam Neeson (playing Rob Roy in the movie by the same name). Filmgoers love watching independent-minded individuals fighting against odds for their freedom and love of their land and society. Both stories end in tragedy.

---

[8] During college I had the great pleasure of living for twelve months in Glasgow and made several visits to the land where the McLennans (MacLennan) lived near the Kyle of Localsh on the road to the Isle of Skye. I would eventually get married in my McLennan Kilt, as my wife was led down the aisle by a Scottish highland bagpiper...one of my fondest memories. Completely irrelevant to this book but thought I would share!

The story of the Scots provides yet another metaphor for us in addressing the change we need to make. The Scottish gradually lost their battle with the English, which eventually led to their loss of independence. To be certain, the Celts were tenacious fighters and cunning on the battlefield. They won some important battles by banding together – clan-to-clan and tribe-to-tribe – to repel a common foe. When joined together, properly led and emboldened by a passion for their land and culture, they were often unbeatable. But between these hard-fought victories, the Scottish clans often fought each other, spilling one another's blood over local feuds. Whether to increase one chieftain's influence over another or through treacherous allegiance with the English, the smaller battles only ever led to short-term gain. In the end, the better organized and consistent English force won out by dividing and using the clans' weaknesses to its advantage. It is a story that has played out across the span of history and groups all over the world could showcase similar stories.

It is an apt metaphor for our struggle in the environmental and the green building movements. While we band together effectively from time to time, we are more often divided and counterproductive. At times we undermine each other and become one another's harshest critics and adversaries. Many forge ahead completely unaware of what others are working on, competing for resources and duplicating the same work instead of collaborating and looking for synergies.

Regardless of how effective we are as individuals, we must become part of a larger, more orchestrated movement in order for our efforts to have a wider-reaching impact that will affect change on the scale required. Great societal challenges are never solved by a single person, regardless of how important some individuals become. The Civil Rights movement was bigger than Dr. King, an understanding of which he himself preached. A movement, by definition, requires a community.

To be successful, we must orchestrate a gathering of all the tribes. The process of bringing allies together should become a single focus point for the efforts of any green warrior. If you are not working on how to collaborate and leverage the work of others, then you are doing the wrong work.

Our "tribes" in this case are wider than ever before, as environmental challenges should truly transcend political parties, religious backgrounds, nationalities and fields of expertise. Changing the tide and the course of civilization is the profound challenge and work for humanity in the decades ahead. We are the tribe, a tribe of humanity, and the battles we face require fighting our own attitudes, inertia, greed and prejudices.

NEW TOOLS FOR A NEW ERA

Twenty-first century green warriors must take up 21st-century peaceable arms. We have an abundance of new tools at our disposal that allow us to communicate with other members of the movement globally and in real time. The web, cell phones, text messages, blogs, tweets, social networking sites and countless other technological tools are all part of an open source environment that has the potential to serve us in a bottom-up and top-down revolution simultaneously. Given the urgency of the issues at hand, our movement must make full use of state-of-the-art communication in order to mobilize. Barack Obama and his team understood this option perfectly, and used these new tools to create a powerful and active community that helped elect him President. Perhaps in doing so, he signaled the end of the last major vestiges of the Civil War that still haunted this country.

Forward-thinking for-profit companies such as Google offer wonderful examples of how to build a business model based on the dual goal of serving the greater good while running a successful enterprise. I am also fascinated by www.WiserEarth.org, which is the first open source network for global social change. More impressive are the thousands of open source communities, where people who have never met each other and likely never will, work collaboratively to solve problems, create new software and use community goodwill and mutual benefit to solve problems. One need only look at Wikipedia to see the potential power of what is possible. While far from perfect, Wikipedia contains hundreds of thousands more entries than the most powerful encyclopedias and private networks. While its accuracy at times can be questionable, it is for the most part surprisingly accurate due to its process of continual evolution and self-policing and it is always more up-to-date and vibrant than Britannica could ever hope to be. Recently, a friend introduced me to the social and animation phenomenon called Second Life, an open source interactive world that is truly global in scope with its own currency, relationships and cities teeming with life. People are learning how to interact and communicate in ways that free them from their current perceived limitations.

In the modern age, the gathering of the tribes must use electronic communication and organization to tackle the challenges we face in the "first life" – the real life on our planet. These tools do not separate us further behind computer screens and false avatars, but facilitate real interactions and deep communication, often face-to-face, neighbor-to-neighbor in ways that have been lost since World War II.[9]

---

[9] I highly recommend that people read Robert Putnam's excellent social analysis called *Bowling Alone: The Collapse and Revival of American Community* (2000).

BLESSED UNREST

I had the privilege of getting to know Paul Hawken back in the late 1990s through Bob Berkebile, which gave me the rare opportunity to learn first-hand about Hawken's work and his revolutionary ideas rather than simply through his writings. I first read his book *The Ecology of Commerce* in 1993. Like many who read it, I was deeply influenced. I was particularly struck by the fact that Hawken, an environmentalist and a capitalist, understands that making a living does not require drawing down the planet's capital. He maintains that it is possible and always preferable to devise market-based solutions that create networks of opportunities that serve the people and the environment at the same time. With the right intentions and a spirit of love and compassion for humanity and creation, powerful things were possible.

In 1999, Hawken published *Natural Capitalism* (co-written by Amory Lovins and L. Hunter Lovins), which serves as an unofficial sequel to *The Ecology of Commerce* and includes powerful examples of commercial scenarios that benefit ecology as well as economy. (We are reminded that both words come from the same Latin root "eco" meaning "house.")

I am not alone in my assertion that Hawken's 2007 release, *Blessed Unrest: How the Largest Movement in the World Came into Being and Why No One Saw it Coming*, is his most important contribution to the cause. The book talks about the explosion of environmental, social justice and community organizations that has quietly emerged over the last couple of decades to become the largest movement in human history. These groups of like-minded individuals now number in the millions and wield enormous influence for just causes throughout the world. There are so many non-governmental organizations that it would take days to list all of them working around the world on behalf of indigenous groups, the poor, the disenfranchised, the uneducated, the exploited, the environment, resources and intersections between all these issues and more. Most amazingly, there was no centralized planning structure that brought these entities together; there is no one leader who runs the show and the majority of the organizations work in silos, unaware of the efforts of groups who work for the same goals. The untapped potential is staggering. Somehow we have to truly unite the tribes globally.

The idea that we are truly not alone in wanting to make significant change happen is palpable when you read Hawken's book, visit Wiser Earth and begin your own investigations of the dozens of groups and individuals you likely have within your own neighborhood or community. Most of these individuals and organizations fly below the radar, doing good work that benefits all of us – often without pay and personal reward. What will it take to truly connect us? Just imagine a city filled with unbelievable musicians who only practiced their instruments independently and never heard one another play. Now imagine the music they could make if they combined their efforts into a symphony.

I am drawn to the teachings of Paul Hawken because he is an optimist while also being a realist who can sit with the pain of our current predicaments. Despite the constant barrage of bad global news, he sees the potential – the rising consciousness – of this powerful movement. He believes that the various branches of the movement will integrate into a powerful force, populated by individuals who care deeply for the human and the planetary condition.

FINDING THE TRAILHEAD

Sometimes, people simply are not ready to participate. They are not quite ready to ask themselves the tough questions about their core values, and to make profound changes in how they do things; they are not ready to start at the beginning – to look inward and understand what they need to change inside themselves. Usually, these folks are caught in old paradigms, and continue to do things the same ways they have always done them even long after it stops feeling right to them. Until people are truly ready to change, they continue to build buildings, develop communities, create partnerships and pursue relationships (with others and themselves) using their old patterns. To those people – whether they are coworkers, peers or possibly close family, parents or spouses – we must be patient and not self-righteous. While we can never give up on these people, even when we desperately need or want their participation in the movement, we can not also force them or guilt them into "migrating" with us until they have gone through their own Zugunruhe for their own reasons.

That, I think, is what defines the spirit of true collaboration, which must always begin with accepting people where they are. When times are hardest and we feel most dire, we must find within ourselves a place of beauty, inspiration and love that can keep us moving forward with a positive attitude, even when we do not always see eye-to-eye with those around us.

My good friend David Eisenberg (himself a green pioneer, poet and green warrior) talks about a concept he calls "finding the trailhead." He notes that any form of deep collaboration requires finding a trailhead – identifying a point of entry or common understanding whereby it is possible to walk together with anyone. Once we are on what he calls "the path of commitment," change is possible. But without a common trailhead, we will never find each other for the trees. The point is that with proper navigation through understanding and empathy, we can steer through the bramble of fear, ignorance and preconceived notions.

Yet, locating the trailhead is only the beginning. Once on the path, we must walk alongside our collaborators and figure out a way to travel forward while continuing to relate to their values and belief systems even as we stay true to our own. (Ideally, they will do the same and usually do when sincerity is evident.) The result is a mutual understanding of all players' unique paths of commitment. Using the trailhead as a metaphor helps rid the collaborative process of the "my way or the highway" types of approaches that tend to bog down partnerships.

All of us should seek our own trailheads with every potential collaborator and not assume or take for granted the gifts and hard lessons we each have to bring. Healthy collaboration helps us offer up our individual strengths while learning from the collective offerings of our colleagues. When done properly and thoughtfully, it can magnify the impact of a few committed individuals for the benefit of the broader community.

The Tragedy of the Commons

We are currently caught in the parable of *The Tragedy of the Commons*. An ancient concept, it was popularized in modern times by Garret Hardin's essay of the same name, published in 1968 in *Science* magazine. Hardin explained the paradox in environmental terms: when groups of individuals act independently for their own selfish interests related to shared environmental resources such as food, water, trees and pasture, they often end up hastening the demise of the shared resource.

Even when presented with the obvious fact that their long-term interests will be destroyed, they continue to act in ways that degrade the resource. The positive impacts of their actions are immediate and benefit them alone, while the negative impacts are shared equally among those who share the resource. This pattern puts a perverse incentive on continuing the behavior until the resource is destroyed. The fisherman who over fishes depletes the overall stocks yet still gets to sell more fish at the market than his competitor. Each fisherman, coming to the same conclusion, over fishes in order to maximize his or her position until the fishing populations crash (as has happened with almost all major fishing grounds and fish populations).

The tragedy is that this kind of problem can be avoided through proper communication, understanding and collaboration – ensuring equality of use and sustainable benefits. The collaboration must be total. One person fishing within his or her quota when everyone else is over fishing does not solve the problem.

The Cascadia Partnership Charter

In my role as CEO of the Cascadia Green Building Council,
I have seen some negative and, unfortunately, unproductive
relationships emerge between individuals who should, by any
rational stretch, be strong allies. These are people with shared
values who are fighting for the same causes, yet seem to devote
more energy to judging one another than they do to reaching
those they are trying to influence. They sometimes forget their
fundamental positions and get caught up in day-to-day issues
and differences, at which point they lose their focus.

After one particularly harsh period, during which I was actually
trying to defuse a situation between one of my staff members and
one of our allies, it occurred to me that we needed some help. We
needed a simple tool to remind our partners and ourselves how
to treat each other; a manifesto of the fundamental spirit of our
collaborative work. So I created Cascadia's partnership charter
to document our intentions.

Now, whenever Cascadia enters a major partnership with any
group, we submit the charter and an accompanying letter. In
essence, it brings all parties to the same starting point; a place of
agreement regarding the spirit of our partnership. This simple
tool has had a transformative effect on many of our relationships.

CASCADIA PARTNERSHIP CHARTER

February 9, 2009

Dear Portland Branch,

At Cascadia we take partnerships very seriously. We've learned through challenging situations that a partnership is not really defined through an MOU, a licensing agreement or a contract. It is instead defined by the quality of our relationships and the spirit of love, compassion and dedication we bring to the collaboration. Our partnerships with any organization are successful only to the extent that the people involved care about each other and for each other.

We are currently living in an age of great change and environmental uncertainty resulting in what could be the most pivotal point in human history – as a result, the changes we need to make are vast and cannot be achieved by disparate, disjointed organizations. Simply-put – we need each other. It is ironic that the biggest barriers we face are not technological or economic, which are so often given as the culprits. They begin with us. The biggest barriers to profound change are attitudinal and relate directly to the quality or lack of quality of the partnerships we create. We are limited primarily by our own capacity to change, or our own inability to recognize the type and scale of changes necessary. Yet, as Mahatma Gandhi once said "we must be the change we wish to see in the world."

This charter is an invitation and a commitment for a deeper, more meaningful partnership where we truly begin to act with an attitude that gives us a fighting chance to make significant progress together. By signing this document we are willing to fully embrace you as a partner and make a firm commitment to your success. As our partner we ask you to sign and commit to us with the same conviction.

Cascadia thanks you in advance for the gift of your time and spirit.

With warmth,

Jason F. McLennan
CEO, Cascadia Region Green Building Council

CASCADIA PARTNERSHIP CHARTER

In forming this partnership we (the undersigned) commit to the following relationship:

1. We promise to say what we mean and mean what we say so you always know where we stand on issues.

2. We promise to look out for your personal and organizational interests and well- being because we are vested in your success.

3. We promise to commit only to the things we truly think we can deliver on and do our best to deliver as promised.

4. We promise to speak up when we disagree rather than going along with something we won't ultimately support. If we say yes, it means yes.

5. When we do disagree we'll approach the subject as your friend, brother or sister and attempt to walk in your shoes and see the issue from your perspective as well as our own.

6. When we need to be critical we promise to do so in a respectful and helpful manner and will speak to you first to honor our partnership.

7. We promise to check our own "baggage" at the door as we recognize everyone brings preconceived notions and expectations to any relationship.

8. We promise to not project our own expectations on you without discussing them and really asking whether the expectation is fair.

9. We promise to communicate rather than assume – to pick up the phone or come by in person if there is ever any confusion or heated issues- e-mail is a poor communication surrogate.

CASCADIA PARTNERSHIP CHARTER

10. We promise to fight to our core for our shared values and put the mission first – before any personal or organizational gain.

11. We pledge to forgive you prior to any transgression as a basic operating philosophy – as we recognize in advance that mistakes happen and sometimes people can't deliver on everything. We don't expect perfection as a condition of our partnership.

12. We promise to give you another chance and a third if needed if mistakes are made.

13. We promise to express our frustration without anger and in a constructive manner.

14. We promise to care about your concerns and your issues, which might be different than ours.

15. We promise to listen to you and to hear out what you are worried about and fearful of.

16. We promise to share and find ways to collaborate wherever possible.

17. We promise to connect you with others we meet or come across that might be important to you.

18. We promise to act with a spirit of love and support towards you, your staff, volunteers and colleagues.

19. We promise to work hard to be successful in the work we collaborate on.

20. We promise to review and recommit to these commitments on a biannual basis.

GWERSI XXVII

Instead of despairing over a lack of progress
towards change,

Reach out and find others who are also working
to create change.

Look for people in other disciplines and for ways
to bring your ideas and expertise together.

This collaboration will inspire you and keep you
positive, grounded and moving forward.

GWERSI XXVIII

The true migration begins not with finding yourself, but with finding others ready to migrate with you.

With each action, look for others with whom to share, learn and collaborate.

Seek common understandings and solutions and make the cornerstone of your vision one that is inclusive, synergistic and open-source.

15

THE POWER OF MYTH AND METAPHOR:

HARNESSING STORYTELLING TO CHANGE MINDS

"We humans live by stories. The key to making a choice for Earth Community is recognizing that the foundation of Empire's power does not lie in its instruments of physical violence. It lies in Empire's ability to control the stories by which we define ourselves and our possibilities in order to perpetuate the myths on which the legitimacy of the dominator relations of Empire depend. To change the human future, we must change our defining stories."

—DAVID KORTEN

Human beings have always used stories to explain the world – we are a race of myth makers and myth believers. Our collective stories, metaphors, myths and parables bind us, free us, imprison us and define us all at once and like nothing else. Each culture has a unique set of myths that inform how it perceives itself, how its members relate to one another and how humans as a species relate to the natural world.

In our culture, parents tell their young children stories that help preserve a sense of magic in the world that perhaps we have lost. The tales are intended to surprise and delight, and help keep alive the feeling of awe derived from the ignorance of how things really work. The Tooth Fairy, Halloween witches, storks bringing babies, leprechauns, rainbows and gold and egg-carrying bunnies populate the stories we hear in our youth and we perpetuate as adults to the next generation. Perhaps no fictional character in our culture is more potent than Santa Claus, the most powerful symbol for the lengths to which our culture collectively goes in order to engage children in the spirit of a certain holiday. The fact that younger generations today tend to associate Christmas more with Saint Nicholas than with the birth of Jesus proves the power and malleability of cultural metaphors to change the original meaning of even sacred rituals. Not surprisingly, in our secular society, many young children in North America recognize such icons as Santa Claus and their corporate counterparts such as Ronald MacDonald and Mickey Mouse more readily than they do Christ, Buddha or other major religious figures.

"A Myth is defined as someone else's religion."
—Joseph Campbell

As adults, we hold onto our love of myth even as we distance ourselves from the idea that our beliefs are based on stories, parables and metaphors. For centuries, the great religions have used stories and parables to provide control and influence over their congregations – including at times royalty and military leaders. Such influence can be dramatic and mythology can be shaped to justify even the most immoral behaviors and excuse acts that run against the original edicts of their faith. (The Crusades serve as a horrific example of killing in the name of God, despite clear direction that believers "shalt not kill.") Secular monarchies, empires and dictatorships also routinely use stories and mythology to shape the direction of their countries and sometimes whole civilizations. One need only look at the Nazis and Stalinist communists to understand what humanity is capable of when captivated by the wrong propagandized mythology. What people "buy into" can shape empires and ravage civilizations and the planet.

While we like to believe ourselves part of an enlightened age, I propose that our collective need to believe in stories has never been more powerful. While modern manifestations of collective mythologies are often more subtle, more shapeless and less tied to the supernatural, they are no less powerful in shaping all aspects of our societies and communities.

CORPORATE AND POLITICAL STORIES

The same strategies used for generations to deceive and refocus human energies are alive and well today. Granted, they are more often less directly and tangibly despicable. But indirectly and over time, they may end up being equally harmful. Big corporations, for example, have transformed "citizens into consumers," weaving networks of stories and mythologies that have led us to accept a system of commerce that rapes the planet and distributes the related costs among the poor and the many for the benefit of the rich and the few. Harmful impact gets externalized, which appears to make the whole mess less messy, at least for those who craft the tales.

As consumers, we rarely blink when we purchase a complex electronic item for ten to one hundred dollars that could never carry such a low price tag if it were made through an environmentally-friendly process by workers who were well paid. Think about it. Take a small appliance like a toaster, made up of several dozen components produced all over the world. If it retails for eighty dollars, that usually means that the retailer paid less than forty dollars. Forty dollars is not a lot of money for something that contains components from twenty different countries and has traveled thousands of miles before it lands on an American shelf. The only way this economic system works for North American consumers is to externalize as many environmental costs as possible and pay people next to nothing in the third world country it was made in. Marketing campaigns tell us what is good for us and for commerce, and help us forget about undesirable practices that for the most part happen "somewhere else". Over time, we begin to demand even lower costs for our goods, further fueling the downward trend and becoming desensitized to the reality.

Mythological tales portraying the "American way of life" and the "American dream" are filled with imagery of the frontier, the entrepreneur, conquering the wilderness, owning land and making one's own way. This idealized portrait is painted on a backdrop of promise – the promise of wealth and prosperity, all of which is considered a God-given right. Unfortunately, we have committed enough to this dream that we have fought wars and established corrupt foreign policies in order to maintain and protect it. People of low- and middle-income support the system that keeps them poor because they too have bought into the myth to the point that they do not question it and indeed they maintain the mostly false hope that one day they will break free and join the ranks of the "haves."

I would go so far as to say that this country's chief export since the mid-20th century has been its stories rather than its goods. We distribute these mythologies elsewhere in order to help our own realities spread to other parts of the world. And it is working. The American way of doing things is becoming increasingly common throughout the planet. People in China and India clamor for car ownership and for the things that we buy without pause, even though doing so will bring further unsustainable strain to the planet. Who can blame them when we have sold them such an evocative image of success? At the same time, our mythologies are gaining us powerful enemies abroad who understand that our way of life has had extreme consequences on theirs.

STORIES GETTING IN THE WAY OF PROGRESS

Every culture ever documented has a "creation myth" and one or more god myths, along with stories that help explain how people relate to the natural world (via weather, geography, food, other species, etcetera). As new information is collected, the myths evolve, get updated or change based on human conflict. In most cases, conquering peoples impose new doctrines upon those whom they have overpowered, and the tales spread.[1] Since the Age of Enlightenment, Western culture has defined itself based on a particularly powerful, yet destructive set of accumulated stories.

Even today, the stories we use to explain the origins of our species continue to make headlines with heated battles over whether our children should learn about evolution or intelligent design taking place in many counties and states.

---

[1] Although in many cases it is the conquered that have a more lasting impact on the culture and beliefs of their conquerers.

Perhaps this is just how we are wired. It is almost impossible for human beings to understand new concepts without explanations coming in the form of stories and metaphors rooted in the past. Fiction, after all, can be much more powerful and moving than non-fiction. Similarly, the best non-fiction is written as a powerful story that conveys a message, a desired outcome and layers of emotion. The best of these tales allow people to suspend their disbelief long enough to associate and identify with the messages being presented.

Savvy marketers understand this model. Harley Davidson promotes freedom and ruggedness more concretely than it sells motorcycles. Apple offers up an appealing and hip counter-culture approach to technology more overtly than it describes the features of its products. It sells a lifestyle.

Embedded within all of these stories are metaphors that help us understand the messages, internalize the meaning and connect the dots, particularly when multiple ideas are presented. The right metaphor is like a key that unlocks multiple doors; utilized properly, a metaphor allows people to fill in missing pieces of a story (with both good and bad results) and aligns people around sets of ideas.

Together, myth and metaphor pose the largest cultural barrier to making profound change. Yet they also present the greatest opportunity for the transformation we seek.

CHOOSING STORIES

"One reason we are in so much trouble is that our modern culture is paradoxically behind the times, still assessing the world the way it did in the nineteenth or even eighteenth centuries: as a place of inexhaustible resources, where man is at the pinnacle of creation, separate from and more important than anything around him."
—David Suzuki

To be successful – to create profound change – we must fully recognize the stories and metaphors we have bought into as individuals. Specifically, we must identify which stories are dangerous and which ones need to be replaced, for the sake of our own health and happiness as well as for the well-being of the planet. All of us, at some level, have bought into some sort of cultural mythology that is keeping us from reaching our greatest potential and allowing us to justify actions and lifestyles that deep down we know are not right. The challenge is to recognize which unhealthy tales we believe and take steps to create a new paradigm. This realization is a critical part of the ongoing migration that defines Zugunruhe.

In the 1970s, the energy crisis woke many people up to the idea that the "cheap oil" rules under which we had operated were simply not sustainable. The environmental movement was just getting its legs and the first modern green buildings began to emerge as a response to the crisis. Granted, the first green buildings (then simply called energy-conserving buildings) were clunky, awkward and sometimes even ugly. The good news for the green movement was that they got built and could provide an early foundation to test valuable ideas such as the integration of photovoltiacs and passive solar into architecture. The bad news was that the so-called establishment labeled them ungainly, expensive, risky and impractical, and as soon as oil prices fell again, most people went back to the same lifestyles and made the same decisions as before. Famously, then president Ronald Reagan took the solar panels off the White House. Only a few people soldiered on, continuing to develop the ideas of green building and paving a trail for all of us who practice today. They did this despite the fact that the "stories" they were telling were at direct odds to the stories told by almost all sectors of society. The eighties and nineties, a dismal time to be green, surrounded people with the celebration of consumerism and the desire for more and larger "supersized" everything. After years of scraping by, early green pioneers are finally becoming vindicated, as it has become obvious that they were right all along.[2] Still, myths about green building persist; stories that sustainable structures are too expensive and strange looking are still rampant. Once ingrained, mythology is hard to shake.

It is now time to free ourselves from these antiquated ideas and replace them with tales of communities and societies banding together to support a healthy and just planet. We must establish a new mythology of what it means to be successful, what "growth" really means and what our proper place in creation should be.

NEW STORIES

Looking ahead, we need to craft new, more holistic stories of our own; stories that help us redefine success, explain the assumptions we make regarding our work and our environment, encapsulate what really matters and clarify our role within our local and global communities in order to build a future that is socially just, culturally rich and ecologically restorative. Some critical thinkers in the green building movement have already begun this process and are telling powerful new stories that are making a significant difference and beginning to reshape the dialogue. Paul Hawken's books, for example, about the role of business and the true role of the market in creating a just planet, contain powerful ideas on the ecology of commerce[3] and how to achieve commercial success while staying true to environmental principles. Several corporations, including

---

[2] Until very recently, even celebrated professors at highly regarded architectural schools dismissed green building as a fad that diminished the art of the craft.

[3] The name of one of his seminal books.

such giants as Interface Carpets, have credited Hawken's words and visions for their environmental transformations.

Visionary architects such as Bill McDonough have captured people's imagination by talking about abundance instead of scarcity. He discusses the possibility of a future material economy that is more "cradle to cradle" than "cradle to grave," as it is infinitely useful and ultimately recycled.

"Our goal is a delightfully diverse, safe, healthy and just world, with clean air, water, soil and power – economically, equitably, ecologically and elegantly enjoyed – period!"
—Bill McDonough

The Janine Benyus book, *Biomimicry,* challenged the metaphor for all our creations. She wrote that nature was the ultimate metaphor, measure and mentor for all of our technologies. She powerfully reminded us of key natural properties that serve as both metaphors and direct guides for how we should live, interact and build.

Nature:

- Runs on sunlight

- Uses only the energy it needs

- Fits form to function

- Recycles everything

- Rewards cooperation

- Banks on diversity

- Demands local expertise

- Curbs excesses within

- Taps the power of limits

My own creation, the Living Building Challenge (LBC),[4] was inspired by Benyus' approach and based on the simple metaphor of a flower. (The LBC calls on the design-build community to leave the mechanistic "building-as-machine" model and evolve to a new standard where buildings function as living things.) To achieve Living Building status, buildings must meet twenty simple, but profound imperatives including such difficult goals as achieving water and energy independence. Its power lies in the simplicity and elegance of its message – clearly defining the endgame of where buildings need to head for true sustainability to be reached. Within only months of launching the most stringent green building program on the planet, several dozen projects emerged, as ambitious architects, institutions and developers sought to be the first to achieve the Living Building protocol. The race is on to build the first living buildings of all building types in every state and province in North America and as of this printing the first certified Living Buildings have emerged.

Similarly, the Pharos labeling program which I co-created with Bill Walsh, aims to provide a holistic overview of the "greenness" and social worthiness of individual building materials and is another metaphor-based initiative. Using a symbolic lighthouse as its primary graphic tool, the Pharos label has the potential to guide consumers and builders toward informed choices by showing them how a given project performs across a wide array of attributes. It "shines a light" on the truth of how most materials are made with little regard for social justice and environmental burdens.[5] It only takes a few moments for people to realize that they are looking at the missing "nutrition-label" for building materials.

---

[4] For more information on the Living Building Challenge, visit www.ilbi.org.

[5] For more information on Pharos, see www.pharosproject.net.

Pharos™

ENVIRONMENT · RESOURCE

SOCIAL · COMMUNITY

HEALTH · POLLUTION

1

2

3

CAUTION: Not all categories on the lens are equal and vary by material and product.

ENERGY
WORST IN CLASS   BEST IN CLASS

WATER

PRODUCT : _____

FUNCTIONAL UNIT : _____

Embodied Energy Content: _____
Embodied Water Content: _____
Recycled Content : PC _____ % PI _____ %
Rapidly Renewable : _____ %
Low VOC Emissions : _____ Y _____ N
Life Expectancy : _____ yrs.
Warranty Period : _____
Take-Back Program : _____
Closed Loop Recyclable : _____ %
Biodegradable : _____ Y _____ N

Made in : _____

CONTAINS :

HIGH HAZARD CONTENTS :

The Pharos Label

I believe Pharos or tools like it that focus on the idea of radical manufacturer to consumer transparency will eventually redefine how materials are discussed and specified in the building industry, ultimately leading to newer, more benign formulations.

FINDING THE STORYTELLER WITHIN

As we go out into the world to make and facilitate change, what new set of stories will we use? How will we develop new mythologies to support a healthy relationship between future generations and their natural surroundings? It is incumbent upon us to create the metaphorical framework for a new American/Canadian/ Chinese/Indian and so on dream; one that starts within each of us and radiates outward. Our very survival depends less on our technological prowess than it does on our skills as storytellers.

Commonly Mis-told Tales

"The worst disease of the world now is probably the ideology of technological heroism, according to which more and more people willingly cause large-scale effects that they do not foresee and that they cannot control."
—WENDELL BERRY

The current set of stories under which our culture operates contains some very dangerous ideas that our children and grandchildren will have to work very hard to overcome. Included here are just a few of the perilous beliefs that have become so commonly accepted because they have been embedded in the stories we have been telling ourselves for years.

- We can and should ship products anywhere on the planet. A global economy is an advanced economy.

- We can and should build our cities and buildings using the same methods and materials anywhere on the planet. An international style, rather than a regional style, is advanced and modern.

- Machines are the future. (The ultimate metaphor for all of our human-made artifacts such as cities, buildings and transportation is the machine-based metaphor.)

- Worrying too much about the future is a waste of time because we will have the technology and know-how to fix

any problem we create. The precautionary principle is
for crazy Malthusians!

- Nature is ours to use as necessary to support our
economy and way of life. There is so much of it – and it is
so strong that we can not possibly do anything wrong.

- Energy is cheap and easy to come by and we will always
have lots of it. Therefore, we should build an economy
based on whatever is cheapest to extract and use and the
market will take care of the rest.

- Capitalism and free markets are the best way to ensure
that everyone does well and they set the cornerstone for
democracy and freedom. The first step is to open up any
country to free enterprise regardless of their social and
humanitarian records since a free market will eventually
set them free.

- We have a God-given right to bend nature to our will.

David Korten and the Importance of Storytelling

Few people have explored the power of stories and their effect on culture and environment more thoroughly than David Korten, a widely read author and thought leader within the green movement. Best known for his book, *When Corporations Rule the World,* Korten reports on corporate globalization and presents practical ideas on how to resist it. He has written for years about the out-of-control power of corporations and the need for the green movement to stand up and demand changes for the sake of sustainability. Most importantly, Korten helps his readers understand how stories can either serve as tools for or barriers against profound change.

In one of his most recent books, *The Great Turning,* Korten shines a powerful light on the mythologies that have shaped who and what we, as a society, believe. He talks about two types of stories: Empire stories (which have governed us in the West for centuries), and Earth Community stories (which must overcome the Empire stories). With his permission, I reprint a few key passages from his book.

EMPIRE STORIES

According to the Empire Security Story:

We live in a dangerous world, filled with evil enemies. Our security depends on the aggressive use of strong police and military forces to control and eliminate criminals, terrorists, and other foreign enemies who hate us for our freedoms.

This story, a favorite of political extremists, equates social order with a strong state able to dominate and control others before they dominate and control us, measures the strength of the state by its police and military powers, and calls us to trust in the wisdom and benevolence of those who command this power. It serves well those who seek to secure the liberty and privilege of a ruling dynasty through coercive means. It is destructive of peace, and the liberty and creativity of the rest of us.

The Empire Meaning Story teaches that:

God created the heavens and the earth in six days, commands humans to go forth to establish dominion over the earth, favors the righteous with wealth and power, and commissions his favored to rule over the poor who justly suffer divine punishment for their sins. We find meaning in obedience to God and his appointed representatives.

This meaning story equates meaning with obedience, affirms a system of patriarchy in which we humans assume the roles of dependent children in relation to rulers who assume the role of strict fathers. It dismisses the victims of imperial domination as inherently unworthy and claims divine right for rulers accountable only to God—actively undermining the mutual responsibility and accountability essential to democracy and community.

You likely noticed the underlying pattern in these imperial stories. They teach us to believe that inequality is good and just, the use of physical force to impose the will of rulers is essential to social order, and wealth and power are a measure of righteousness. Each contrasts starkly with the corresponding Earth Community story.

EARTH COMMUNITY STORIES

According to the Earth Community Prosperity Story:

Healthy children, families, communities and living systems are the measure of real wealth. Mutual caring is the primary currency of healthy communities. The processes of economic growth consume the social and natural capital that are the foundation of real wealth and expropriate the labor of the working class to increase the power and privilege of an elite owning class. We can end poverty and heal the environment only by reallocating material resources from rich to poor and from life destructive to life nurturing uses. We increase the real wealth of the community by investing resources in growing the social capital of caring relationships and the natural capital of healthy ecosystems. Markets have an essential role in healthy economic life, but markets must have rules to secure community interests, maintain equity, and favor human-scale local businesses that honor community values and serve community needs.

According to the Earth Community Security Story:

Crime and war are indicators of failed relationships. Strong, caring communities are the foundation of both freedom and security. Mutual trust and caring nurture the moral and emotional maturity essential to responsible freedom, provide resilience in times of crisis, and break the imperial cycle of exploitation and violence that is the primary source of our insecurity. Retribution against wrongdoers perpetuates violence. Healing troubled relationships removes the root cause of violence.

The Earth Community Meaning Story teaches that:

All of Creation is the manifestation of a great spiritual intelligence engaged in an ever-unfolding journey of discovery in search of unrealized possibilities. Each species is a participant in that journey. Those that find their place of service to the whole prosper; those that fail perish. Human meaning comes through finding our place of service as co-creators in a conscious, self-organizing living cosmos. Healthy societies nurture the higher potentials of our higher nature essential to finding and fulfilling our place of service to the whole. Human violence, greed, and exploitation are manifestations of our human failure to actualize the potentials of our higher nature. We humans now face our final examination to determine whether we are a species worthy of survival. A passing grade will require a sweeping cultural and institutional transformation aimed at unleashing the potentials we have allowed Empire to suppress for far too long.

GWERSI XXIX

Each of us identifies with cultural myths and metaphors told to us since we were young.

Seek awareness of which stories and mythologies still govern your thinking, and ask why.

All mythologies can be replaced with new stories that support your goals.

GWERSI XXX

In teaching others, look for innovative ways to deliver the message.

Every idea or lesson is more easily grasped through the right metaphor.

Understand that by reaching people through stories, the greatest change is made possible.

16

CONCLUSION:
STARTING YOUR MIGRATION TO A BETTER WORLD

"Keep away from people who belittle your ambitions. Small people always do that, but the really great make you feel that you, too, can become great."

—MARK TWAIN

"The one important thing I have learned over the years is the difference between taking one's work seriously and taking one's self seriously. The first is imperative, and the second is disastrous."

—MARGARET FONTEY

I stood in quiet anticipation as the marsh spread out below me. Thousands of birds had gathered, with large groups intermittently rising and circling only to light again on the water's surface. An intricate dance. Poetry in flight and the restless beginning of a mystical process that has stretched back thousands of years from this place – a place of rocks, low shrubs and marsh on the great Canadian Shield – that would lead the birds far to the south to their winter homes in Alabama, Georgia, Mississippi and Louisiana. But for now, each one was preparing: eating, resting in fits and starts, and circling. Zugunruhe.

This year was different. Many were returning home to coastlines that had seen a huge oil-related disaster: the BP Deepwater spill. While the repercussions were largely invisible, the food chain at all strata of ocean and shoreline depths had been affected. Will they return next summer healthy or changed in some critical way?

The next morning I too took flight – first leaving my hometown in Sudbury, Ontario, then getting on a plane in Toronto and flying several thousand miles west to SeaTac airport in Seattle. My journey was measured in hours, not days and instead of being active, I rested semi-comfortably on a less-than-full flight. I was going through e-mails previously downloaded. A friend e-mailed me to tell me that he had just lost his job and that there was nowhere to find one. This great recession continued to make people struggle. I scanned my e-mails more. Another friend told me she had just passed her LEED Accreditation exam and was excited to finally get started in the green design field, yet she worried that the economy would force people to be concerned more with keeping down costs than with sustainability. I paused in thought. This vicissitude was only the beginning of much bigger changes to come.

So here's the deal, my friend: Firstly, thank you for journeying with me through the pages of this book. More importantly, thank you for your awareness about what's going on. Things are going to change a great deal over the next couple of decades and the rate of change is only going to increase. We will be required to be more resilient, more effective and simply stronger in order to face these challenges head-on and lead our communities to a healthy and truly sustainable place.

 I know you feel it like I do. The huge global population explosion. The pressure on the few wild systems that remain intact. The end of cheap energy and the systems propping up civilizations that depend on it. The increasing challenges brought on by climate change, more extreme weather and the potential runaway scenarios that scientists predict. All of this change occurs in the context of a heavily-armed and polarized planet.

As I say in many of my talks, this is the first year of the last decade to make significant change and we have not yet moved the needle. *So the change is coming to us.* And it will fall to us to be ready and effective, to show the kind of collective leadership that has been lacking. Our civilization is about to change course and the world we grew up with – which we came to believe was "normal" – is beginning its de-evolution. A new paradigm will await the next generation and creating a graceful transition in the now is the most important task our species has ever faced.

On bad days, I don't think we are going to make it. But for the sake of my children – and children everywhere – I know it's time to shake these feelings and move forward. As discussed earlier, we need to learn to sit with uncomfortable knowledge and draw motivation and action from it rather than be paralyzed or delusional.

Heady stuff. You see why I didn't start the book this way! The ideas shared in *Zugunruhe* have helped me in my own journey and I hope a few can help you in yours. You can make a difference, and you already are making one. While we all need to start by "getting our collective shit together," no great migration happens alone. When it is time, well, we go together.

On that note, I would like the last words of this book not to be my own, but rather the collective wisdom of some fellow green warriors who inspire me and many others to be the change we wish to see in the world. All of them are leaders and visionaries and offer words of wisdom to anyone on a personal migration. What better way to end one "chapter" and begin another? Enjoy the journey, my friend, and thank you for sharing *Zugunruhe* with me.

– Jason F. McLennan
   Bainbridge Island, Washington

BOB BERKEBILE

I have found that a trend toward white or no hair increases the incidence of requests for advice. Not that I have any to offer. But I enjoy the questions and often agree to help search for answers. When I first met Jason, it was clear that he had a lot of questions and that adding his inquisitive mind to our firm was the right decision for us and for him. I was certain it would be interesting, but I had no clue what our dialogue of discovery would bring.

At the time, a team from BNIM that included Jason and me were traveling frequently to Bozeman, Montana. We were designing a national demonstration project at Montana State University that was funded by a grant from the National Institute of Standards and Technology (NIST). The project, and the relationships that emerged throughout the process, evolved to have far greater impact than our client, NIST, or any of us could have imagined.

The NIST grant sought a new benchmark for energy efficiency in buildings. Just prior to Jason joining us, I had requested additional funding that would allow us to develop strategies for improving the ecological and economic systems in the Gallatin Valley as a result of the construction and operation of this research lab. NIST generously doubled our grant, and with the additional funding we were able to assemble an impressive team of consultants including one of the co-founders and the founding chairman of USGBC as well as two future chairs and at least seven who would eventually serve on the board.

Because the project was in design concurrent with the conceptualization of the LEED rating system, concepts for the project and LEED often were inseparable.

It was a very special team of creative thought leaders. But I noticed that our new intern, Jason, had more questions than any of our scientists or experts. And Jason's questions would continue into the night. We started rooming together to facilitate our dialogue, and it didn't take long before the conversations broke beyond the project and design strategies to other unanswerable questions about life and the universe. I was accustomed to questions from students and younger colleagues, but this was different. A repetitive theme at the core of his questions was how he could be more effective, have more impact, create more change. I had no answers for him; in fact I hadn't been able to answer these questions satisfactorily for myself. So I would often share what my mentors had shared with me:

Robert Mueller (UN Undersecretary General) and Leon Shenandoah (Iroquois chief) had both encouraged me to, "Listen to the truth, or the Great Spirit within." Joseph Campbell referred to it as "following your bliss," and Buckminster Fuller called it "design intuition." Bucky also said, "Bob, the only way to make significant change is to make the thing you are trying to change obsolete."

I would share these experiences and answer Jason's "why" questions until sunrise or fatigue interrupted. Jason shared stories about his family and his experience participating in the environmental transformation of Sudbury. But mostly we explored the potential for changing existing design, community and economic doctrine. It was a collaborative dialogue of discovery, and it continues to this day.

Since those first enjoyable conversations with Jason, I have learned much from/with him and my colleagues, our clients and a long list of collaborators that, thankfully, is growing exponentially. But the world looks very different to me today than it did when I met Jason. Science has proven that our obsolete design and community doctrines are threatening our very future, and the time for changing that doctrine is very short if we care about our children.

So now when someone asks for advice I continue to share my mentors' advice and I often add something from Vaclav Havel: "Hope is not the conviction that something will turn out well, but the certainty that something makes sense, regardless of how it turns out."

When preparing new planning and design teams, I share the urgency I feel for accelerating change and some advice from an Aboriginal activist group: "If you have come to help me, you are wasting your time. But if your liberation is bound with mine, then let us work together." I also share seven lessons I have learned working on projects from Antarctica to Haiti:

1. Restorative design and community building is a team sport.

2. Creative planning and design are more process than destination.

3. Honor the wisdom of all participants and recognize that it is a dialogue of discovery. (Listening has priority over speaking, and when speaking, utilize words that can be heard – positive and inclusive trumps negative and divisive, and avoid judgmental words.)

4. Read the science, but act from your heart.

5. I'm still evolving, and I strive to be the change I want to see.

6. Celebrate everyone and their successes whenever possible.

7. Beauty, love and fun always trump facts and performance in growing capacity.

This weekend in New Orleans, on the fifth anniversary of Katrina, I was reminded of some advice from Albert Einstein: "Learn from yesterday, live for today, hope for tomorrow."

SIM VAN DER RYN

In a recent Commencement Speech at Stanford University, Apple founder Steve Jobs made the point that, "you can't connect the dots looking forward, only looking backwards..." In his fifteen-minute talk, Jobs told three stories about his life. He was adopted at birth, he never went to college and he stumbled into computers through a class in calligraphy, and he recently recovered from an almost fatal illness. You can't plan your life as a programmed series of connected dots. The only thing that is certain is uncertainty, and your ability to follow your heart and intuition. Remember that " intuition" is defined as "direct perception independent of any reasoning process." So intuition is not a rational mental process that one can map out.

Jason, my partner Francine and I had dinner after a talk I gave in Seattle last year. We talked about how we had discovered the paths we were on. For Jason, growing up in an Ontario mining town where the rivers ran red with radioactive waste seemed to be a transformative experience. For me, it was our Dutch Jewish family fleeing Holland shortly before the Nazis invaded our country and learning five years later that most of our family that stayed there died in the holocaust. At our dinner, we didn't talk about at what point our transformative experience shaped what we've each done in our lives. For me, I couldn't make sense of it until I wrote my last book, *Design For Life*. I was writing about my early years and realized, "If you escape one holocaust, you don't want to be part of creating a larger one".

As a Berkeley professor, I interviewed graduate school applicants. Noting their excellent grade point averages and reading their statements of purpose, I always asked each one to tell me what they really loved doing. Many of these bright people froze like a deer in the headlights, stuttering while they tried to figure out the correct answer to my simple question. For those who couldn't come up with one thing they really loved doing, I would sadly mark a "reject" on my evaluation. Was I being too mean? Again, as Steve Jobs told the Stanford audience of achievers, "Love what you do…..first you have to find what you love…if today were the last day in your life would you being doing what you do?" Last week I heard visionary activist Caroline Casey talk in our community center. She said, "Imagination lays the tracks for the reality train to follow" and also quipped this little bit of Native American wisdom: "If we don't change our direction we're likely to end up where we're headed."

This connects with "zugunruhe" – a migration from a culture of destruction which forty years ago one of my mentors described as "burning down the house of life in order to toast marshmallows" – and the potential for a great turning towards an integral culture which makes transparent the whole human journey we have traveled the forty thousand years or so we've been around, a journey where all forms of life are connected to support life and not destroy it and ourselves.

I've lived on this planet seventy-five years and on my wall is a quote attributed to Gandhi, "Live every day as though it is your last, learn every day as though you will live forever." Good advice I continue to follow.

DAVID KORTEN

For the many millions of us working to create a better world, it is easy to feel discouraged by the seeming insignificance of even major individual successes relative to the scale of the problems we face as a nation and a species. Consumed by the details and challenges of our daily engagements, we may easily lose sight of the big picture of the powerful social dynamic to which our work is contributing.

Step back from time to time; take a breath, look out beyond the immediate horizon to bring that big picture back into perspective. Reflect in awe and wonder at the power of the larger social dynamic to which your work contributes.

Successful social movements are emergent, evolving, radically self-organizing, and involve the dedicated efforts of many people, each finding the role that best uses his or her gifts and passions. Their scope and their success may not, at first, be readily apparent. Social movements grow and evolve around framing ideas and mutually supportive relationships instead of through top-down direction. New ideas gain traction, or not, depending on what works for those involved in the movement.

The organism, not the machine, provides the appropriate metaphor. The relevant knowledge resides not in the heads of outside experts but in the heads of the people who populate the system. The challenge is to help them recognize, organize and use that knowledge in ever more effective ways.

So how do you know whether your work is contributing to a big-picture outcome? If you can answer yes to any one of the following five questions, then be assured that it is.

- Does it help discredit a false cultural story fabricated to legitimize relationships of domination and exploitation and to replace it with a true story describing unrealized possibilities for creating a human future of living buildings and living communities?

- Is it connecting others of the movement's millions of leaders who didn't previously know one another, helping them find common cause and build relationships of mutual trust that allow them to speak honestly from their hearts and to know that they can call on one another for support when needed?

- Is it creating and expanding liberated social spaces in which people experience the freedom and support to experiment with living the creative, cooperative, self-organizing relationships of the new story they seek to bring into the larger culture?

- Is it providing a public demonstration of the possibilities of the future you seek?

- Is it mobilizing support for a beneficial rule change that supports practices consistent with the living building/living community challenge?

These are useful guidelines for setting both individual and group priorities. Bear in mind that there is no magic bullet solution when dealing with complex social change and no one is going to make it happen on their own. Do not be discouraged if the world looks much the same today despite your special and heroic effort yesterday. It took five thousand years to create the mess we humans are in today. It will take more than a few days to set it right. [1]

[1] Adapted from David C. Korten, Agenda for a New Economy, 2nd edition, 2010 with permission.

THOMAS CRUM

The cloud does not insist on its form

The wave does not force its way over the ocean

So why should you clutch so tightly your little map?

Haven Trevino

Recently, I did a six-day Magic on the River trip down the
Middle Fork of the Salmon River in Idaho. The Middle Fork
is one of the true wild rivers in the U.S. with no man-made
dams or motorized boats allowed along the entire 100-plus
mile stretch. The river did the teaching: the principles of flow,
impermanence, life and mystery were imprinted upon us with
every bend and canyon.

Floating down the river, we would look up to see an eagle
soaring, look to the side on the canyon rocks and see a big horn
sheep, or look down and see trout shimmering under the water.
And then – poof! It was all gone as a new bend in the river
arrived, with maybe deer, or a bear, or a waterfall misting over
us from so high up that the sunlight and mist created a magical
celestial shower. And then another bend, another moment.

In all that flow of beauty there was also destruction: hundreds
of trees knocked down by avalanches or mudslides and jammed
into rocks below; acres of burned forests from lightning strikes;
dead salmon too tired to swim the final miles to spawn. The
water was quiet and peaceful one moment, then roaring with
fury the next. And yet it seemed – through both life and death

– so purposeful, so majestic, so harmonious. For me, it was nature's way of teaching the warrior spirit.

I define the warrior spirit as the total commitment to become fully alive. Sounds like something we would all aspire to, doesn't it? The difficulty comes when we realize that to become fully alive we must cut through the ego and its stories and dramas, the veils that the ego uses to define us and provide some semblance, however false, of security. The river has no need to play such games. As the canyon pours down boulders, trees and mud, she responds in flow, acceptance and aliveness.

Our own lives produce an endless supply of boulders as well; difficult work situations, tumultuous relationships, emotional turmoil, physical illnesses or injuries that challenge our sense of OKness. The warrior spirit is the courage to accept those "boulders" with centered equanimity and continue flowing on.

When we have learned to stay awake in the difficult, fearful times rather than medicating them away or running to the comfort of our old dramas, our same old stories, something profound happens. Not enlightenment or deep peace, at least, not at first. It's even more discomfort. We may feel even more physical pain, gut-wrenching emotion and mental anguish – because being awake and present begins to strip away all the ego trappings that we have acquired over these many years, the ones that give us a sense of groundedness, safety, of OKness. And that loss can be painful and scary.

But, just when we're lying on our backs in the blood and tears of it all, with nothing to hold onto – bang! (or maybe it's just a whisper) – we discover we're still here, and somehow we're flowing a little more freely inside. The river does not insist on its form. Why should we?

If we can learn to appreciate, with centered equanimity, the twists and turns, the rapids and eddies, of our life, a little more of the Mystery will seep in. Peace and joy flow into our being; compassion and kindness flow out. And, as a result, everything begins to change, from our perspective to our communication, to the effectiveness of our actions. And, if there is anything needed more than all the others in changing to a greener world, it is compassion and kindness. Because that is what will transform our relationships and our relationship to this Mother Earth. This is the true warrior spirit.[2]

[2] Author of Three Deep Breaths (Berrett and Kohler), Magic of Conflict and Journey to Center (Simon and Schuster). For more information on Tom and his programs, please see his website, www.thomascrum.com.

NADAV MALIN

Action Empowered by Uncertainty

As a researcher and journalist, I'm motivated by the search for truth. Not capital "T" Truth – I'll get to that later. Simply the best available information about a particular issue.

As an activist, I'm interested in telling a story that will affect people's behavior and choices. I believe that we as a society have to change how we do things, and I want to inspire people to make those changes.

These two agendas – research and activism – are sometimes in conflict. Change is best motivated by unambiguous, compelling messages with simple calls to action. But the truth about a situation is rarely simple, and always subject to change as new facts and perspectives emerge.

So I often face the question of "what message do I want to convey?" in an article, a speech, a conversation. I try to tune my message to the situation and meet the audience on their own terms. Sometimes people don't want to be fully informed – they want a simple answer that they can run with and go on to the next thing.

Often, however, people want to make up their own mind. They are mistrustful of those who want to tell them what to do, and prefer to hear the full story and come to their own conclusions. For them, providing detail and nuance and even conflicting information is a way to earn their trust, after which it's easier to steer them in the direction I think is best.

When I find myself seriously perturbed about a particular problem, I lean towards the side of convincing people to take my view – which generally involves simplifying the message and glossing over complexities.

Then I reflect on what I've said, or I hear another person doing the same kind of convincing, and it doesn't feel right. I hear the one-sidedness of their arguments, and I'm compelled to complete the picture by introducing the counter-arguments and nuances. But no amount of nuance can convey the entire picture, nor could I ever really know enough to understand all the aspects.

This world we inhabit is miraculous and infinitely complex. As any good scientist knows, there are no "laws" of nature – only hypotheses to be tested until they are found lacking and replaced by more advanced hypotheses. Everything we claim to know about a situation is only our best guess, based on a sliver of the potentially relevant evidence.

That might seem paralyzing – if I don't really know anything for sure, how can I act decisively to address the problems that I perceive? In practice, however, I have found it liberating – at those moments when I act decisively while recognizing my less-than-perfect knowledge, I become more effective, not less. I've relinquished the pressure of believing I know the absolute right thing, and carry a sense of wonder, even into strong action. Acting without a dogmatic belief in the rightness my actions – that's a manifestation of the deeper Truth that I seek.

KATH WILLIAMS

The quest for the "meaning of life" seems to possess many individuals. This rumination supposedly marks a deep thinker and profound wisdom comes from the unearthed "answers." The change agents in my life have shown me a different path, a much simpler approach. It is *carpe diem*, or in the case of sustainability, seize the daily opportunities to lead change.

Sustainability is like perfection; we'll never get there. There will always be new challenges to face in this complex universe. So the individual actions we take and the paths we choose on a daily basis – and we do make choices – either contribute to or detract from the overall progress toward this unattainable goal. Which is not to say the path to sustainability is the wrong one, just because the goal is not within our reach. Striving for perfection makes everything and everyone better. The migration toward sustainability does and will make a difference in and of itself.

From my life experiences, the role of the individual was outlined in the three maxims on the ancient Temple of Apollo at Delphi –"Know Thyself," "Nothing in Excess" and "A Pledge, the ruin is near." The Seven Sages' brevity is easily expounded upon on the path to sustainability. Change agents know their strengths and weaknesses and almost innately find their place to contribute. It isn't about location; it's about individuals having their own sense of place. They know themselves and where they are and they take action at every opportunity.

Excess is the fundamental flaw in the decisions of much of society – past and present, with the same dangerous focus being the driver of the future. This is mankind's greatest challenge, to undo the impact of excess in all aspects of life – environmental, economic, and personal.

The third maxim is about promises, particularly in regard to contracts and money, according to Euripides. The Sages do not mean to abstain from gaining and using wealth, but they are advising to this day against strong decisions based on money alone, against eagerness in making promises and against decisions that cannot be recalled or changed.

Simple constructs for making a difference as we work down the path toward sustainability? About as simple as becoming perfect. An appropriate fit to one's personal "zugunruhe"? Absolutely.

DAVID EISENBERG

This book is about both a restless inner migration sparked by a deep caring and about how to navigate the uncharted territory this type of journey requires. Among the many things I might share in this small space, what seems most vital are those that might help place and hold your work in a context large enough for such a journey.

Jason talked about trim tabs as a metaphor – the importance of leverage and finding leverage points where relatively small actions can have profound effects. Aside from a warning about humility in the face of ever-present unintended consequences, I'd like to suggest another metaphor related to water and boats – that of sailing. I'm not a sailor, but I am fascinated by the reality that it's possible to sail into the wind and against the current, using the forces flowing, seemingly, in the wrong direction for power. This requires being able to hold in your mind a larger map that includes where you are, where you're trying to go, which way the wind is blowing, sometimes which way the current is flowing, and a level of mastery of technique that enables progress toward your destination, though for only brief and occasional moments are you actually pointed directly toward your goal. It's well worth the time spent to familiarize yourself with the concepts used in sailing so they can inform your work.

I also want to point out a trap awaiting those focused on measurement but lacking big enough mental maps in the realm of creating systemic change. There are many truisms about the importance of measurement and quantification. There are a few warnings as well, including the sign that hung over Einstein's desk: "Not everything that counts can be counted, and not everything that can be counted counts." It is all too common to measure the wrong things to incredible degrees of accuracy while ignoring the very existence of others of much greater significance. We also tend to discount anything we think too difficult or impossible to measure. Economists are notorious for this because most have been trained to view their partial map of reality as containing everything worth measuring. The rest are "externalities" (uneconomic things such as natural systems, health, families, generosity) deemed not important enough to measure. The key is measuring more than just the things; measure their relationships, whole systems effects, lifecycles, flows over time, quality, vitality, love. Some are not measurable with the tools we've been taught to use. But humans have extraordinary capabilities to see and sense things that matter. We need all these ways of knowing, including what you know in your heart, in your gut, in your soul.

And here's one last observation for staying sane over time while working toward huge goals and living with the feeling that we're constantly falling short and running out of time. If you've read this book to this point, you're almost certainly interested in having your work and your life account for something of value, but that means being able to persist. So, heres a pattern that I had to repeat many times before I acknowledged it as a pattern that was robbing me and others of our ability to fully reclaim and recycle the energy from the successes in our projects. It goes like this: a new project emerges with wonderful, aspirational goals and enthusiasm all around. As the project proceeds many compromises are made. At the end, although the project easily surpasses most other projects, our primary experience tends to be of the gap between where we started out and where we ended up. Our successes often feel like failures. The tension from that gap is important. But as important, is the conscious acknowledgment and celebration of what was actually accomplished. Without it, we burn out.

So, we need a big enough map with a long enough timeline, a large enough set of goals and some fun to stay healthy, sane and productive for the long haul. Or, maybe it's as simple as this: the way to subvert the dominant paradigm is to have more fun than they do and make sure they know it.

KATHLEEN O'BRIEN

When my youngest son and his wife were expecting their first child, he asked me for my advice on parenting. I wondered why he, of all people, would be asking me this, since he knew firsthand of my imperfections in this regard. However, I did share with him what I had learned. "Scott, for me it has to be simple: Always admit when you make a mistake and always let your child know you love him." ("Him" turned out to be a "her," by the way – my beautiful granddaughter, Ellie!)

The reasoning for the second half of my maternal advice – to make sure Scott's child felt loved – should be obvious to anyone. But why is it so important to admit mistakes? First, it's about being honest. No one is perfect, and to act like one could be is to perpetuate a dangerous fantasy that we might actually be so. It is living a lie, and asking our children to live in denial of what they intuitively know. Second, it's about being teachable. If we admit mistakes, and particularly if we see them in proper proportion (not too big, not too small) and in their proper perspective (not an occasion for blame but an opportunity to learn) we can actually grow from them. To put it simply, we mature. By admitting our mistakes to our children, we show them how they can grow.

I believe both pieces of advice work just as well for adults desiring to be a cause for sustainable change. Act out of love, not judgment. Don't be self-righteous bores. It's tedious, and it doesn't work. But also love your fellows enough to be genuine. Sometimes love looks less like a hug, and more like a correction.

And be teachable, so you can learn and so others can witness that and open themselves to the opportunities that may be open to us all. Jason encourages us to use the right side of our brain, to be what he calls a polymath, to resist temporal dilution and parasitics, and to go outside of our comfort zone through deep structural shifts. This absolutely requires the willingness to make big, glorious and sometimes public mistakes. Yup, and it doesn't feel terrific sometimes. But the more we do this the more we learn to be gentler on ourselves (and others) when we (or they) err, and the less likely we are to stick to the conventions that will kill us if we cling to them. We'll be better mentors, and better recipients of mentorship.

I mentioned earlier that admitting mistakes is also a matter of honesty. Facing the truth about our personal impacts – at home and out in the world – is extremely important. The creative tension it causes – by revealing the dissonance between our core values and our actions – is a necessary pre-condition for change. And we cannot expect our fellows to change if we don't. So, honesty and love. Not easy.

For me, getting to this place has required inner work. What this work looks like for you will be unique to your situation, so I'd best not give any advice here. Besides, there are plenty of others much more suited to do so. Getting here has also required a commitment to continued and disciplined study. Rather late in my life, I took a masters at Antioch University Seattle in Environment and Community, and as part of that program was mentored in independent study by Janine Benyus, who I understand is writing the preface of this book, and inspired its title. In that precious experience she offered me far more than I can describe in this small space, but one thing is especially relevant that I want to mention: the idea of being precise in our articulation of sustainable concepts, the necessity to back our green building solutions with rigorous study. So it is not enough to be teachable; we need to commit to continuous education that has depth and breadth. So perhaps it is best we keep our left brain engaged along with our right brain. God Bless.

SANDY WIGGINS

We human beings are the foam on the advancing wave of
evolution in our little corner of the universe, and we are
far more gifted than we allow ourselves to believe. We
are each born with the capacity to be a discrete, self-aware
intelligence. We are also each born with the capacity to be
connected to and part of the vast collective intelligence of a
living universe. With that capacity comes the ability to know
things that transcend the culturally activated voice in our head.
Unfortunately, we are trained from birth to disbelieve and
suppress this connection and the innate ability that comes with
it. Unlearning that training is our great work. Establishing
that connection is our great hope.

Every day we are presented with countless opportunities to act
on our connection to each other and the rest of creation. Usually
these opportunities float by us and we shrug them off, afraid to
pay attention to our "intuition" or "inner voice" – afraid to pay
attention to what we really know to be true. But when we do pay
attention and act, our lives and the lives of those around us are
always changed for the better. These are the actions that give
our lives meaning and fulfillment, and they are the acts that
inspire others. They are acts of leadership.

Real leadership takes courage, which is the ability to act in
spite of fear. Acting on my inner voice has often required me to
summon enormous courage because of the cultural conditioning
that has taught me to suppress it. It is really uncomfortable
when your heart is in your throat and the voice in your head

is shouting for you to sit still and keep your mouth shut. But I have never been sorry when I've summoned the courage to ignore that noise, listen to my inner voice, and act on it. As a result, I have learned to pay attention to that particular kind of discomfort as a sign that I am on the right path.

Fortunately, unlearning our cultural prejudice to listen only to that "rational" voice in our head, which tends to separate us from each other and prompts us to put our personal interest above our collective interest, gets easier with practice. As I've learned to yield my separateness to connection and listen to intuition, my life has become more purposeful, my work has had greater impact, and I've become much more effective as a leader. I've learned that the thoughts and words of my inner voice resonate with others in spite of my fear that they might be rejected or ridiculed. It is our common voice. It emanates from our connection, and we all crave connection and the meaning that comes with it.

The most effective way to facilitate change is to help others discover that they too are connected and empower them to listen to their inner voice. It puts them on the ladder of awareness. Once done, just get out of the way.

Your own experience from the world of the voice in your head is a powerful asset. It opens doors and gives you the credibility and language to speak to others' listening. Recently, I found myself in front of one hundred "C-level" executives from as many companies speaking about the economics of sustainability. Halfway through my well-prepared talk, my inner voice was prompting me to go off script into deeper territory while the voice in my head argued that I'd be a laughing stock. I listened to my inner voice and ended up with a conga line of business leaders waiting to talk to me about what I'd shared. You can't change the way others act, but you can help them change the mindset from which their actions emanate.

APPENDIX A
GWERSI APPENDIX

I

// PAGE 60

Find a mentor, not a hero.

In fact, seek many.

We all walk in the shadows of others and must begin by acknowledging and honoring those who have taught us.

To be effective, one must continually search for mentorship

Regardless of age or years of experience.

Be humble and learn from those who teach you.

II

// PAGE 61

If you know one thing, teach that.

All of us should see teaching others as part of our own growth

As it brings clarity and coherence to one's own understanding

While lifting up and advancing others.

It is a gift of spirit and a chance to test ideas.

Anyone can be a teacher with immense value.

It only requires knowing just one thing that someone else does not.

Be brave and confident,

For your insights have value and beauty.

III

// PAGE 77

In nature, diversity breeds resilience.

The same is true for our own resilience as people.

Therefore, seek first to become well-rounded in knowledge and training.

Less important are degrees and letters and the need to specialize.

Continually look for experiences outside of your current field of understanding, as the health of our inner dimensions – happiness, creativity and peace – are dependent upon being connected to an expanding network of experiences.

IV

// PAGE 78

Chart your path to polymathy.

Learning should be a meandering path – book-to-book, experience-to-experience.

It should be charted generally but not absolutely, and it should jump field-to-field,

Discipline-to-discipline as new knowledge is needed.

The notion of "that is not my area" is outdated. It is always in our field if we care to learn.

V

// PAGE 95

Look deeply for habits, patterns and systems that support all aspects of your life – where you live, what you do, how you travel and what you eat – and explore the possibility of a complete change, not an incremental one.

Strive for each action to reinforce the kind of impact you wish to have.

Find holistic solutions that simultaneously solve multiple things you want to address.

It is your life.

You are not trapped in your reality.

VI

// PAGE 96

In your business or work,

Find opportunities to codify environmental improvements.

Reexamine standard procedures, rules of thumb and corporate policies.

Institutionalized restoration can work as easily as institutionalized degradation.

Challenge and question.

Redefine.

VII

// PAGE 114

Turn thinking on its head.

When stuck in a problem, change the paradigm by turning it upside down.

Think consciously of how your opposite would react and cultivate both your left and right brain modes of problem solving.

Stretch out of your comfort zone so that you are ready to change dramatically when it is most important.

VIII

// PAGE 115

Be brave and look for the ideal solution in every endeavor.

It is not too much to ask for solutions to life's challenges that are healthy, environmentally sound and economically wise.

Slow down, aim for simplicity and make each decision count.

Practice mindfulness.

IX

// PAGE 116

Take time to "make risotto" in all aspects of life.

Add flair and beauty to the tasks you face and revel in your ability to put your personal stamp on your creations.

Have fun with the little jobs you do, which make you better able to appreciate the more significant accomplishments that come along.

Enjoy the present, for that is all we have.

X

// PAGE 134

Learn to tell the truth to yourself as nobody has ever done.

Be neither too hard nor too soft, just realistic and optimistic.

Ask yourself how the most fair and wise judge would judge you, instead of the harsh critic or doubter.

Internalize this voice in your assessments and recognize the ego for what it is:

A false prophet within our heads.

XI

// PAGE 135

What has been done is done; it is in the past,

Available for lessons, but not to be changed.

So do not dwell, but let go, forgive, move on, make amends, find peace,

As you can not go forward while staring backwards into the gloom.

XII

// PAGE 136

You can not become something greater if you do not know where you are today or exactly where you should be when you arrive.

So set goals for your career, for your knowledge and for what you want to achieve.

Then project yourself into that reality and begin to act

(without taking yourself too seriously) like that reality is in the now.

Be both humble and confident, aware of what you know and do not know.

Be hungry to learn and change.

XIII

// PAGE 149

Look for opportunities to test yourself.

Be willing to fail, not just once but as many times as necessary.

For it is in the failure that true success is found.

Understanding why something works

Is best done through learning how and why it does not.

XIV

// PAGE 150

When something does not go as originally planned, embrace the change

And recognize that there is great value in having assumptions and ideas proven wrong.

True growth comes from learning how to change

Rather than doing anything possible not to be wrong or to keep things the same.

Only the fool views success as never having been wrong.

XV

// PAGE 168

To create change requires leading with love.

Extend compassion and understanding as you work with others

And have patience for things to unfold as they should.

Instead of judging, try supporting and you will be amazed at the results.

XVI

// PAGE 169

Working to help others and create change begins by helping yourself.

It is impossible to lead with love without loving yourself.

So treat yourself well and appreciate what you bring to the world,

Regardless of how small or large.

XVII

// PAGE 185

In any endeavor, scale the effort of your work to the effort required for success.

Accept that sometimes your "best" varies under different conditions.

Do not overthink or overdo.

Learning balance and restraint without harsh internal judgment is a fundamental requirement of true success.

Perfection comes not when it is sought, but when it is not.

XVIII

// PAGE 186

Release your ideas and innovations to the world when they are
3/4-baked.

Learn when to stop and invite others to contribute and collaborate.

Reject the urge to constantly refine and improve until something is
perfect before sharing.

Chasing perfection is a fool's errand.

The chance for perfection grows by letting go,

Not by hanging on.

XIX

// PAGE 200

Embrace conflict as a necessary and valuable part of change.

Do not avoid it, hide from it or seek it recklessly, but step into it
when necessary.

Use conflict as inertia in which to move from one paradigm to
another.

XX

// PAGE 201

Do not view conflict as an opportunity to win or defeat an opponent.

Instead, view it as an opportunity to test mutual assumptions, ideas
and policies,

Arriving at a place that is healthier, more profound and more true.

XXI

// PAGE 220

Developing rules of thumb for things you do is fine,

As long as the rules do not become sacred.

Test assumptions often and be open to new possibilities when assumptions are wrong.

Formulate, test, reformulate, test.

Then repeat.

XXII

// PAGE 221

When placed in a new situation or even a familiar one, do not assume that you know the answer.

Find a way to measure and learn directly what is happening.

Intuitive knowledge is strengthened through a deep understanding of reality.

Measure and analyze.

XXIII

// PAGE 234

When ready to act,

First look to understand how your actions, skills and contributions can do the most good.

Harness the works of others.

Look for ways to leverage change,

And for opportunities for interventions that bring cascading effects.

XXIV

// PAGE 235

Regardless of where you are in your career,

There are always opportunities to make change.

Look for them

And try to find places to intervene where you can leverage your skills and knowledge.

Do not hesitate.

Begin.

XXV

// PAGE 248

Spending too much time pondering how something should be accomplished can be as destructive as spending too little.

The systems we use are not the result.

Therefore, spend the majority of your energy on the actual effort

Rather than the approach to the effort.

XXVI

// PAGE 249

If a given approach is not working, then change it.

If it is only working somewhat, then tweak it.

If it works as intended, then stick with it – with both eyes open.

Become separate from "how" you do things and you may become better acquainted with what you are doing and why.

XXVII

// PAGE 273

Instead of despairing over a lack of progress towards change,

Reach out and find others who are also working to create change.

Look for people in other disciplines and for ways to bring your ideas and expertise together.

This connection will inspire you and keep you positive, grounded and moving forward.

XXVIII

// PAGE 274

The true migration begins not with finding yourself, but with finding others ready to migrate with you.

With each action, look for others with whom to share, learn and collaborate.

Seek common understandings and solutions and make the cornerstone of your vision one that is inclusive, synergistic and open source.

XXIX

// PAGE 295

Each of us identifies with cultural myths and metaphors told to us since we were young.

Seek awareness of which stories and mythologies still govern your thinking, and ask why.

All mythologies can be replaced with new stories that support your goals.

XXX

// PAGE 296

In teaching others, look for innovative ways to deliver the message.

Every idea or lesson is more easily grasped through the right metaphor.

Understand that by reaching people through stories, the greatest change is made possible.

APPENDIX B

THE NEW – GREENWARRIOR READING LIST

"Books are the bees, which carry the quickening pollen from
one to another mind."

—JAMES RUSSELL LOWELL

SOME THOUGHTS:

In my last book, *The Philosophy of Sustainable Design* I created a reading list – I called it the Green Warrior Reading List. It contained a motley collection of books that I had found particularly useful to me in my own journey of discovery – and it was my hope that I could introduce a few of these to those reading my book as well. As it turns out, the Green Warrior Reading list has found its way into a lot of hands. People, as it turns out, like lists.

So here is another one. Updated. Green Warrior Reading List Redux. Some of the titles are the same, some are new. All of them are powerful and important.

Just read them, okay?

AGENDA FOR A NEW ECONOMY - FROM PHANTOM WEALTH
TO REAL WEALTH
David C. Korten, Berrett-Koehler Publishers – 2009

BIOMIMICRY, INNOVATION INSPIRED BY NATURE
Janine M. Benyus, William Morrow and Co. – 1997

BLESSED UNREST - HOW THE LARGEST MOVEMENT IN THE
WORLD CAME INTO BEING AND WHY NO ONE SAW IT COMING
Paul Hawken, Viking – 2007

COLLAPSE - HOW SOCIETIES CHOOSE TO FAIL OR SUCCEED
Jared Diamond, Penguin – 2005

CONFRONTING COLLAPSE - THE CRISIS OF ENERGY AND MONEY
IN A POST PEAK OIL WORLD
Michael C. Ruppert, Chelsea Green Publishing – 2009

CRADLE TO CRADLE: REMAKING THE WAY WE MAKE THINGS
William McDonough and Michael Braungart, North Point Press – 2002

EAARTH - MAKING A LIFE ON A TOUGH NEW PLANET
Bill McKibben, Henry Holt – 2010

THE GREAT TURNING: FROM EMPIRE TO EARTH COMMUNITY
David C. Korten, Berrett-Koehler Publishers 2007

THE LONG EMERGENCY: SURVIVING THE END OF OIL, CLIMATE
CHANGE, AND OTHER CONVERGING CATASTROPHES OF THE
TWENTY-FIRST CENTURY
James Howard Kunstler, Grove Press – 2006

THE MAGIC OF CONFLICT
Thomas F. Crum, Touchstone Press – 1987

THE MIRACLE OF MINDFULNESS
Thich Nhat Hanh, Beacon Press – 1999

THE OMNIVORE'S DILEMMA – A NATURAL HISTORY OF FOUR MEALS
Michael Pollan, Penguin – 2007

OUR CHOICE, A PLAN TO SOLVE THE CLIMATE CRISIS
Al Gore, Melcher Media – 2009

THE PHILOSOPHY OF SUSTAINABLE DESIGN
Jason F. McLennan, Ecotone Publishing – 2004

THE POWER OF MYTH
Joseph Campbell and Bill Moyer, Anchor – 1991

THE SACRED BALANCE – REDISCOVERING OUR PLACE IN NATURE
David Suzuki, Prometheus Books – 1998

THREE DEEP BREATHS – FINDING POWER AND PURPOSE IN A
STRESSED OUT WORLD
Thomas F. Crum, Berrett-Koehler Publishers – 2009

C

APPENDIX C
ABOUT THE AUTHORS

MARY ADAM THOMAS

Mary Adam Thomas is a writer whose commitment to environmental issues began in earnest when she used her allowance money to buy a "Let's Recycle" coloring book in first grade. She has written, edited and consulted on a variety of guidebooks, editorial articles and educational materials in her 25-year career, and her work has appeared in numerous national and regional publications. Mary lives with her husband and two children in the Seattle area, where the natural beauty manages to thrill and humble her on a daily basis.

Working closely with Jason, she helped bring structure and polish to the manuscript.

JASON F. MCLENNAN

Considered one of the most influential individuals in the green building movement today, Jason F. McLennan's work has made a strong impact on the shape and direction of green building in the United States and Canada and he is a much sought after presenter and consultant on a wide variety of green building and sustainability topics around the world.

McLennan serves as the CEO of the Cascadia Green Building Council, the Pacific Northwest's leading organization in the field of green building and sustainable development and he is also the CEO of the International Living Building Institute. He is the founder and creator of the *Living Building Challenge*, an international green building program, and co-creator of *Pharos*, the most advanced building material rating system in North America.

His work in the sustainable design field has been published or reviewed in dozens of journals, magazines conference proceedings and books including *Architecture, Architectural Record, Dwell, Plenty, Metropolis, NY Times, The Globe and Mail, The World and I, Ecostructure, Greensource, Arcade and Environmental Design and Construction Magazine*. He is the author of four books; *The Philosophy of Sustainable Design, The Dumb Architect's Guide to Glazing Selection, The Ecological Engineer* and *Zugunruhe*. The *Philosophy of Sustainable Design* is currently used as a textbook in over seventy universities and colleges and is distributed widely throughout Europe, North America and Asia.

Jason is a former Principal at BNIM Architects, one of the founders of the green design movement in the United States, where he worked on many of the leading high performance projects in the country including LEED Platinum, Gold and zero-energy projects. At BNIM he created the building science team known as Elements, which set new standards for energy and resource efficiency on many of its projects in various building types. Jason has won numerous awards including a national Canadian Green Building Champion award and he was a finalist for the prestigious Buckminster Fuller Award.

Jason was born and raised in Ontario, Canada, was educated in Oregon, Kansas and Glasgow, Scotland and now resides on Bainbridge Island in Washington with his wife Tracy, three sons Julian, Declan and Aidan, and daughter Rowan.

Vist Jason's website at **jasonmclennan.com**.

Visit our website:

zugunruhe.net

To learn more about the book and to
share your zugunruhe experience!

wanted. Enough gold would be his to re-make his life. He would be given new clothes and a berth to Canada or Louisiana, both places where French was spoken and he could start again. A wine merchant from Bordeaux, a ship's captain from Nice, a fisherman from Brittany . . . He could be any of those things or anything else he chose. Men were less fussy in the colonies about lineage. So long as he didn't claim to be noble, or pretend he came from one of the richer merchant families, he would be safe.

This drunken man stared at me. In his eyes I saw the horror of his last five years and wondered if he was too deep into degradation to save himself by telling me the truth. He asked, because who wouldn't, what I wanted in return. I imagine he knew it had to do with the *Angélique*, for there was little else remarkable about him. I explained I wanted to know the truth about his crossing the Bay of Bengal in a tiny boat on raging seas. That I would tell no one else and would bind myself by oath to this. I left my real reason for hunting him down until later and I doubt he ever knew what it was. He simply thought I wanted to know if he'd eaten human flesh.

I wanted to know if it tasted closer to beef, pork or mutton.

The man had eaten human flesh. On the third day, ravaged by hunger, when a ship's boy died, the remaining men looked at each other and the decision went unspoken. One of them simply pulled out his pocket knife and began filleting. The sharks got the guts and bones but the men ate everything else. That was the only time and the only victim, and since the boy was dead, the man asked, what harm had really been done? He looked so desperate that I shrugged and said that was a question for the priests but I would have done the same. And he looked at me to see if I was mocking him and then wrung my hand.

He sailed that night, still drunk but now dressed and shaved and with a passport signed by Jerome that made the captain of the ship he took think he was a radical with connections being allowed to go into exile. Before he left he told me his answer. The meat was tender and easily digestible but bland. It could have done with cooking. And it could have done with seasoning. At the very least it needed black pepper. His understanding of food was too crude to tell me if one cut had tasted better than another.

'Ignore the noise,' I tell Tigris, who keeps freezing her position every time there is a thud or a crash outside. From the sound of it men are battering at the main door and a couple of the side doors. They'll find the doors inside locked as well, which will no doubt upset them. 'Go back to sleep.' But she is too restless and I have to leave her there twitching her great tail while I go downstairs.

I always knew it would come to this. Well, perhaps I suspected in the darkest part of myself, that part we keep hidden from our lovers and our children, and often from ourselves because who wants to admit to himself that he is a monster? Everything I can eat, I have eaten. Every taste I can find, I have found. My notebooks, like my experiences, are extensive but they are incomplete. The dead boy lies where I left him, under the shelf with the Parmareggio. His body has cooled in the previous twenty-four hours and the stone of the larder floor has kept him fresh. 'Meat,' I tell myself, 'is simply meat.'

The words fill my head but fail to convince. It is with an elemental sense of sacrament that I cut the clothes from the boy's body and slice strips of flesh from his buttocks and back. The meat from the shoulder is pale like pork, the meat from the buttocks a little darker but not so dark it could be mistaken for venison or beef. I think carefully about how the meat should be cooked, and in the end I opt for simplicity. This is partly out of respect for my ingredients, and partly because, while I can ignore the mob beyond my doors, I'm aware enough of them to know that marinating meat for hours is not open to me.

Hacking free a chunk of Parmareggio, I smash it into fragments with a meat hammer and use the same hammer to flatten the strip of buttock, then crumble stale *pain campagne* and mix the breadcrumbs with the crumbled cheese, adding black pepper, because I tend to add black pepper to everything, and some shredded sage. I dip the flattened meat into a saucer of beaten egg, shake off the excess and dredge it through the Parmareggio mix. As I heat butter in two pans, I shred an apple. The back, sliced fine, I fry simply, without any seasoning at all. It tastes like pork. The buttock cooks quickly, no more than four or five minutes each side, and tastes as I would expect—of sage and black pepper and a good Italian cheese. The shredded apple cuts through its richness nicely.

The tastes of France are changing and we are the last of the banquet. After us, the table will be swept clear as surely as the Chinese plates I use will be smashed by the men and women at my door. A new meal will be laid for them, and the first course will taste pure and clean after what has gone before. I write up my final notes, close the book and smile. My work is done. All that remains now is to end this story as it should be ended; and to do that I need to go upstairs again, to my chamber and then to my study. In my chamber I wash as well I can in the cold water of a jug on the side. Stripping off my clothes, I stand naked on a Persian carpet and scrub every part of me. My body is old and wizened, my arms thinner than I remember and my belly small but low. Fearing that I haven't scrubbed myself thoroughly enough, I find a second jug in another room and wash myself again, removing my wig to wipe sweat from my scalp. I shave my head quickly and rinse it as if readying for a fresh wig, but leave my head bare. This will have to do. Finding the silk banyan Manon bought me with her own money, I drape it over my frame and look round my room. I took Virginie on that bed, Manon too. I have waited out fevers and written letters there to my son and reluctant daughter. It has, in its way, been the centre of my little world.

Tigris looks up as I enter my study, her head to one side as she waits for my voice, but I give her only silence. The noise of the sans-culottes is louder now. They are inside the chateau, outraged at finding all the doors from the hall locked. I hope that I have left enough time and decide I have. It would have been good to be able to say a proper goodbye to Tigris but then what would be the point of washing so thoroughly? And I should have done it earlier if I wanted to do it at all.

Now, I think, *do it now.* But first there is this to say.

This is where I have to stop writing and let you imagine the rest.

Putting down the pen I pick up the razor I used to shave my head and check the edge, already knowing it is sharp. Then I check that my study door is locked and slip the robe from my shoulders and return to my chair, pulling it a little further into the middle of the room. I'm sitting naked in my chair with the razor in my hand, and Tigris is restless and growing upset. Her tail twitches and her eyes flick in irritation at the noise outside and the silence in here. Opening the razor, I watch it gleam in the candlelight, because it's getting dark now and I've lit a candle. Virginie liked candles, Manon also. Women do. I smile, but not sadly. I've lived too long and been too lucky to die sad.

Tigris and I have shared what came to me from Versailles, and the offal from the bullocks killed to feed guests at my chateau. It occurs to me, what should have occurred to me before this: she is my closest companion. They say every man— and, for all I know, every woman—has one great love. I have always thought Virginie was mine, and Manon the peace that came after. Now I wonder if Tigris is not the greatest of my loves. The only one that's really lasted. Men are killed for tasting human flesh and so are tigers. I have tasted this flesh, and

Tigris has not. It will not matter to her if this is a meal she has eaten before in the way it matters to me. But she is hungry and I am ready.

There is courage in resignation but what I do now takes little courage. If I had free choice of how to end my life, this is how I would have chosen that it ends. Years ago I made a *ragoût* from meat cut from Tigris's mother's flank. The meat needed slow cooking for several hours to make it tender, and strong seasoning to make its sourness palatable, but I fried it first with onions and that seems to work for everything from tiger to rat.

Now it is Tigris's turn. The poor animal is hungry and I can see no reason why she should not have one last meal. Drawing the razor diagonally across my wrist so that blood wells but I don't bleed out too fast, I let blood drip to the carpet and watch Tigris's nose twitch. She freezes for a second the way she always does when she smells food. She's puzzled. She thinks it's me in here with her, but she's no longer entirely sure. Most of my smell is gone and I'm not talking to her as I would usually do, and now there's the smell of blood, and she's hungry. I at least have been hungry my entire life. I cut again a second time and a third, wincing at the pain, which is sharper than I had imagined. The fur along her back has risen now. Her head has turned to face me directly and she sinks low to the ground. I know what she looks like resting. This is not Tigris resting.

We are here, where we were always destined to be.

Some of this book is written on paper, some of it is simply the wash of my memories, much of it you have filled in for yourself. I thank you for listening to the ghost of a life now gone from a world that is dying. And though it pains me to believe it, deserves to die. The mob will ransack my chateau, rebuild it in time and as I've already said, one of them will become me. I wish it were different but suspect this is the truth of it. I want, more than anything, to say goodbye to Tigris. I want this more than I want to say goodbye to Manon or Hélène or my son. It cannot be. Gripping the razor one final time, I dig deep into my flesh in a vertical cut that opens an artery in the second before Tigris pounces. I fed on her mother, she feeds on me. Justice is served and the circle closed. I would live it all again.

ENDNOTES

Note 1
This work, reputedly the journal of Jean-Marie, *soi-disant* marquis d'Aumout, was found among the possessions of Citizen Duras, mayor of Limoges, following the execution of the Citizen Mayor for treason.

Note 2
Returned to Admiral Laurant d'Aumout, marquis d'Aumout, trusted confidant of l'empereur, on the orders of the president of the General Council of the Gironde.

ACKNOWLEDGMENTS

I'd like to thank my agent Jonny Geller at Curtis Brown, who stayed up one night to read the first draft of a novel then called *Taste;* Francis Bickmore, Editorial Director of Canongate, who telephoned part way through reading the newly renamed *Master of the Menagerie,* to say he loved the characters and would probably bid but wasn't mad about the title; Lorraine McCann, for a stunningly good copy edit of what had become *The Last Banquet;* and finally, Sam Baker, for whom this book was written.

I jotted down the novel's outline in a café over fifteen years ago, on a strip of paper torn from a napkin. (By which time Sam and I'd known each other for ten years and been married five.) I folded the strip into the back of a notebook, knowing I wasn't grown up enough or good enough to write it. Over the following fifteen years I took it out twice, deciding both times I still wasn't ready. At the start of this year I went hunting for the notebook, and with Sam's encouragement started writing. This is the result.

Jonathan Grimwood December 2012

ABOUT THE AUTHOR

Jonathan Grimwood has written for *The Guardian*, *The Times*, *The Telegraph* and *The Independent* and numerous other magazines and newspapers. *The Last Banquet* is his first work of literary fiction. He divides his time between London and Winchester.